Other books by Jeffrey G. Allen, J.D., C.P.C.

HOW TO TURN AN INTERVIEW INTO A JOB
(also available on audiocassette)

FINDING THE RIGHT JOB AT MIDLIFE

THE PLACEMENT STRATEGY HANDBOOK

THE EMPLOYEE TERMINATION HANDBOOK

PLACEMENT MANAGEMENT

SURVIVING CORPORATE DOWNSIZING

THE COMPLETE Q&A JOB INTERVIEW BOOK

THE PERFECT JOB REFERENCE

JEFF ALLEN'S BEST: GET THE INTERVIEW

JEFF ALLEN'S BEST: WIN THE JOB

Jeff Allen's Best:
The Resume

Jeffrey G. Allen, J.D., C.P.C.

John Wiley & Sons, Inc.

New York • Chichester • Brisbane • Toronto • Singapore

Library of Congress Cataloging-in-Publication Data

Allen, Jeffrey G., 1943—
    Jeff Allen's best: the resume / Jeffrey G. Allen.
      p. cm.
    Includes bibliographical references.
    ISBN 0-471-52537-5. ISBN 0-471-52536-7 (pbk.)
    1. Résumés (Employment)   I. Title.
    HF5383.A563   1990   90-12217
    650.14—dc20   CIP

Printed in the United States of America

90 91   10 9 8 7 6 5 4 3 2 1

For information about our audio products, write us at:
Newbridge Book Clubs, 3000 Cindel Drive, Delran, NJ 08370

To the countless number of personnel consultants and jobseekers whose successes fill the pages of this series. May your "best" instruct and inspire countless others to succeed.

With appreciation . . .

*To my wife, Bev;
to our daughter, Angela;
to an editor's editor, Mike Hamilton,
    who conceived the series;
and to Louann Werksma,
    who assisted with its research and development.*

You definitely keep me at

"Jeff Allen's best!"

About the Author

Jeffrey G. Allen, J.D., C.P.C., is America's leading placement attorney and Director of the National Placement Law Center in Los Angeles. Experience as a certified placement counselor, personnel manager, and professional negotiator uniquely qualifies him to write this breakthrough three-part series on techniques that will result in getting and winning the maximum number of job interviews.

Mr. Allen is the author of more bestselling books in the career field than anyone else. Among them are *How to Turn an Interview into a Job*, *Finding the Right Job at Midlife*, *The Placement Strategy Handbook*, *Placement Management*, *The Complete Q&A Job Interview Book*, and *The Perfect Job Reference*. He writes a nationally syndicated column entitled "Placements and the Law," conducts seminars, and is regularly featured in television, radio, and newspaper interviews.

Mr. Allen has been appointed Special Advisor to the American Employment Association, is General Counsel to the California Association of Personnel Consultants, and is nationally recognized as the foremost authority in the specialty of placement law.

Contents

Chapter 3 Special Problems   **63**

Chapter 4 Video Resumes   **77**

Chapter 5 Sample Resumes   **85**

Jeff Allen's Best:
The Resume

Introduction

Almost 25 years have passed since I began helping people get hired.

I can still feel the thrill of my second placement. My *first* was getting myself hired—as a corporate recruiter. But getting someone *else* hired convinced me a job interview is nothing more than a screen test. An act.

The hiring process will never change. It depends almost completely on the "actor factor." If you get the "casting director's" attention, know your lines, perfect your delivery, and dress for the part, you'll get hired. If you don't, you won't. One big break. No retake.

After my starting role as a corporate recruiter, I spent almost a decade behind a personnel "director's" desk, conducting countless casting calls in hundreds of hiring halls. Interviewing hopeful hirees of every age, stage, and wage, every day (and night—in my sleep). I followed their trials and errors, successes and failures, hits and bombs.

I never viewed that second placement as "beginner's luck." No self-respecting recruiter would. They tell you a lot of reasons why they're successful, but luck isn't among them. After using the techniques in *Jeff Allen's Best*, you'll agree. There's a systematic, consistent, predictable way for anyone to get hired—almost anywhere.

If you look through other "career" books on the shelf, you'll see how "secret" the formula still is. Each author suggests a different approach. Look long enough, and you'll find that half contradict the other half. Some are philosophical, others motivational, and still others personal. Judging by the number of books available on the topic, you'd think everyone who ever got a job is an "expert" on how to get one.

In 1983, Simon & Schuster approached me to write *How to Turn an Interview into a Job*. Its vice-president and senior editor had received a command from the president: "Get that guy!" Nobody knew how the techniques were developed, but they heard how powerfully they worked. I remember the VP's exact words: "We sure can help a lot of people with this book." He was right. We sure did. Probably millions by now. Their success stories are playing on corporate "stages" around the world. They're starring in the roles they do so well. Receiving rave reviews. Writing their own tickets.

Now I specialize in placement law. Thousands of recruiters call and write the National Placement Law Center every year to discuss their placements. Thousands of jobseekers call to report on their successes. "Seconds" become superstars, their careers straight up, their futures assured. Our work continues, as we constantly refine the openers, deliveries, and scripts. But the audience preferences never change. The reaction is always the same: rave reviews. Only more predictably and consistently.

Getting and winning interviews is easy and fun once you know the way. Only the theaters and audiences change—the places and faces—never the reactions. You only need to learn the techniques once, and you're set for life.

I know. You think "background," qualifications," or "experience" have something to do with getting hired. You're right— not about the *job*, though. About *getting* the job! The director only knows what you show. That's why the actor factor is so "critical."

Through the years, I developed the only measure of jobgetting that counts: the *interview-to-offer ratio*. If you ask enough people, you'll find it averages twelve to one. It takes *twelve* interviews for the average person to get *one* job offer. That means for every person who intuitively knows how to get hired every time (or uses the techniques in this series), some walking wounded is limping into his or her *twenty-fourth* interview. For every two people who get the part on their first screen test, there's someone being carried into his or her *forty-eighth*! Destroyed, not employed.

"Almost chosen" doesn't count. Either you're in or you're out. When you're hot, you're hot. And when you're *not*—"Don't call us, we'll call you."

After a while, these folks live with a self-fulfilling prophecy: rejection. They might as well just call the interviewer and say, "I'm cancelling the interview. Your time is too valuable to waste with me." They're destined to flub their lines from the time the first board claps.

Tragic. Even more tragic when that interview-to-offer ratio will tumble down for *anyone* who'll just use the three books that comprise *Jeff Allen's Best*. The techniques I share for writing your resume, getting an interview, and winning the interview aren't philosophical, motivational, or personal. They're the ones that work every time the curtain goes up. Start ad-libbing, and you'll spend your career making a career out of making a career. If something works, it's in this three-part miniseries. If it doesn't, it's not.

I've long since proven that the best person for the job is someone who can get hired. That's because the people who get the leading roles are the people who are promoted faster, have more self-esteem, and bounce back from the ravages of corporate life faster and higher than anyone else.

So, let's get busy. No more "extra" status. No more understudy roles. No more "bit parts," either. Nuthin' to hit but the heights. Your name in lights. I'll be your coach, manager, and even your agent for a while. Come with me into the winners' world of work. Through the back entrance, in the elevator, up to the office with the star on the door.

The techniques in the three books in this series will get you interviewed and lower the interview-to-offer ratio to around *three* to one. Not because I want them to, not because you need them to, but because they're based on a quarter-century of trial and error. The same way every breakthrough since the dawn of civilization has occurred. Soon you'll see that exploring your career world and discovering yourself in the process is more enlightening, more exciting, and even more enjoyable than all the silver screen scenarios you'll ever watch.

You need training in three specific areas to get hired in a target job—writing your resume, getting interviews, and interviewing to obtain job offers. In this volume, we'll discuss resume tips.

Chapter

1

General Rules

The resume is essential in any thorough career plan, for two reasons. Writing a resume is:

Practice for a Polished Performance

Disciplining yourself to develop a supercharged resume is a crucial ingredient in preparing for the interview. To create a powerful resume, you must examine your past in detail. Only when you *know* yourself can you *sell* yourself to others. Preparing your resume teaches you how to match your experience with the requirements of the job you want now. A resume is also:

A Marketing Device

Some career counselors advise trying to arrange an interview without a resume. However, *over 90 percent* of all interviews occur through one. There's no evidence that the remaining 10 percent are "better" jobs, either. Even if they were, you'd need a resume to get hired.

The resume is your paper profile on a page. It is an art form that should represent you effectively in the few words and little space given. That is why so many resumes are ineffective. The job seekers they profile never learned what was necessary to get interest—and interviews.

A resume that just list dates, titles, and employers is like a listing of credits at the end of a movie. It doesn't get reviewed. All that work, preparation, and rehearsal—and the audience walks out while it's playing. No review, no reaction, no reason to reply. Even a "no interest" letter is rarely sent.

Because it is so important to your career, your resume should be the central theme of your career marketing and advertising campaign. It's the preview that gets your audience interested. From there, your interview performance will result in offers.

As you follow the steps recommended to create a winning resume, remember to write your resume as if it were the preview. It is.

DEVELOPING THE CONTENT

1. Begin by taking inventory.

Carefully, completely, critically—and *in writing*. Using the form on the next page, start with your employment history, and *write down* every job you've held. Write the title and a simple sentence describing the function. Include volunteer and community service jobs.

My inventory began with a job scooping ice cream, and by the time it ended I was undoubtedly the original one-minute manager. To explore all your options, be as thorough as possible.

2. Don't disregard volunteer work.

If you are applying for management positions, civic and other experience can testify to leadership, supervisory, and motivational skills. If you are a woman reentering the work force after a long absence, volunteer work is an important indication of your skills and effectiveness. Anyone who has done volunteer work knows how much more skill is required when you lack paycheck power. The hiring authority is probably among them.

JOB INVENTORY

Dates		Job Title	Company/Organization
From	To		
___	___	_____	_____
___	___	_____	_____
___	___	_____	_____
___	___	_____	_____
___	___	_____	_____
___	___	_____	_____
___	___	_____	_____
___	___	_____	_____
___	___	_____	_____
___	___	_____	_____
___	___	_____	_____
___	___	_____	_____
___	___	_____	_____
___	___	_____	_____

3. Summarize each position held.

After listing your (paid and unpaid) positions, use a form like the one on the next page (you're welcome to copy it), make as many copies as you have jobs listed, and complete one for each item in your list.

Keep your completed job summaries in one place—a notebook or binder is handiest—and refer to them as you begin to build the structure of your resume.

This is not a memory exercise. You're not writing a script. That would put any "director" to sleep. You are inventorying your experience. Since you are largely the product of your experience, each of your former activities affects your current attitudes, goals, and marketability.

While your part-time jobs in high school or college may not seem important, they reveal significant facts about you. Did you work to help pay your own expenses? That's an early indicator of a strong sense of responsibility. Did you work to buy your first car? The ability to set a goal and achieve it showed itself here. Your past is the key to your future.

Notice how my job summary form allowed more space for significant *results* than it did for *responsibilities*. What you were *supposed* to do is far less important than what you *actually* did. Think carefully about your achievements.

The first time through, your lists may be incomplete, out of order, and unclear. With time you will bring it all into sharp focus. Revise your lists as you remember the details. You will be sensitizing yourself to the kind of job you want.

Individual Job Summary

Job No. _____

Date: From: _____ , 19 ___   to   _____ , 19 ___ .

Company Name: _____

Address: _____

_____

Telephone: _____

Reported to: _____

Potential references still employed there: _____

_____

Significant responsibilities: _____

_____

_____

Significant results (in descending order of importance):

1. _____

2. _____

3. _____

4. _____

5. _____

4. Ask yourself the following questions:

- What are my primary attributes?
- What are my primary liabilities?
- Which of my past jobs (or duties within jobs) did I like most?
- Which of my achievements are sources of the greatest pride and satisfaction?
- Am I happier in a large or small organization?
- Am I a team player or do I require autonomy?
- Do I enjoy supervising and motivating others?
- Do I like to work with people or with things?
- Do I like the security of a regular salary or the incentive of a commission/bonus system?
- Do I like to travel?

These questions must be answered before you begin writing your resume. Answering them honestly now will help you emphasize what you like in a job. They help you write the right resume for you because they're based on an unalterable law of human nature:

We do best what we like most, and we like most what we do best.

As I said, your past really *is* the key to your future.

With your inventory completed and duties prioritized, it's time to consider the content of the resume.

CREATING THE CONTENT

5. Target your resume to the job.

Theoretically (and practically, if you use a word processor), you can target each resume to the job you want. This maximizes the match of your qualifications, abilities, and achievements to those sought by the employer.

While such a strategy might mean a rewrite each time out, we're not talking about any small reward. It could mean hundreds of thousands—maybe even millions—of dollars more in your pocket over time. Hardly a sacrifice for a lifetime of fulfillment and happiness.

Of course, if you're targeting your resume each time to a specific company and position, you'll probably have to forego the typeset/printed variety—unless you have access to a desktop publishing system and laser printer.

6. Start with a career summary.

At the top of your resume, right after your name, address, and phone number, should be a superstar summary of your qualifications. In a few concise lines, state your major attributes. If you've done it right, it will rivet the reader's eyes and get your resume on top of the "qualified" pile.

7. Summarize your experience, with the most recent employer and position first.

Whether you are a generalist or a specialist, your resume can be written in several different ways. Working backwards from the kinds of positions you want will help you focus on the areas of emphasis. They'll probably be similar to what you've written on the Individual Job Summary form. Listing or summarizing similar responsibilities is acceptable, but you must be *concise.*

When you start with your most recent position, you are writing a "chronological" resume. It's the best way to go—all the way to the top.

Some resume experts advise a "functional" resume, which generalizes your duties and allows you to choose from among your experiences to focus on the target job. But, because interviewers are accustomed to application forms with job experience in chronological sequence, the narrative that a functional resume recites turns them off. To them, they're "flunctional"— foreign, forsaken, and forgotten.

Besides, it is almost impossible to draft a functional resume without looking like you're hiding the truth, or sliding past an undesirable work history. Stick to the chronological method, but combine or omit short-term employment. There is no reason for you to tell everything, anyway. After all, why bother to see the movie if the preview tells it all?

8. If a strict chronological approach won't work for you, use a "combination" approach.

The combination resume mixes features from both the chronological and functional styles. It's a way to combine the flexibility
of the functional with the specifics of the chronological. It allows
you to emphasize certain kinds of experience that are more
applicable to the position you are seeking.

In drafting a combination resume, however, you must pay
close attention to its structure and "time line." People read
resumes looking for a sense of history, years in a position, and so
forth.

9. Keep it short—no more than one page.

An ounce of image is worth a pound of performance.

Resist the temptation to clutter your resume with detailed
information. Details don't sell. Would you buy the insurance if
the company sent you the policy first? Of course not. You
wouldn't buy most books after you'd read them, either. Besides,
overworked personnelers instinctively screen out resumes
longer than one page.

However, a resume targeted to a decision maker, in some
circumstances and in some professions, can be as long as two
pages. But that's a resume customized to a specific situation. I'll
discuss those exceptions later. For a preview resume, usually
sent to a personnel department or a post office box, stick to one
page.

Tom Jackson, in his book *The Perfect Resume* offers this additional exception to his otherwise rigid one-page rule:

> If you have written a variety of articles or books, received an impressive list of honors or awards, obtained a dozen or so patents, or worked on a number of recognizable products, . . . consider an *addendum* to your resume in the form of a separate listing of these specific activities. The important thing is to make it clear that your resume *ends* on the first page, and that the attachment is more of a laundry list of examples rather than part of the page-one story.
>
> At the bottom of the first sheet, try a statement like: "List of publications attached," so that it's clear that if the recruiter wishes he can get the full story without turning to the addendum.[1]

10. Put the "hook" at the top.

Good scriptwriters hook and hold the audience's attention early.

In spite of that proven jobgetting technique, authors are still writing books with resume formats that are 20 years out of date. The top half is overloaded with less important data: personal statistics, education, or objective.

Make your main points early. After your name, address, and telephone number comes the summary—a concise, compelling statement that sums up your career and ability to assist the employer.

Then, immediately launch into the main body of your

"preview"—the show-stopping copy, arranged chronologically, that reveals what you've accomplished, accentuates your effectiveness, and holds your audience's interest.

11. List only the more recent positions.

If you want your resume read, stick to the essentials only—the ones that will really impress.

And make it timely. Learn to cut from the bottom. Employers want to know how great you will be tomorrow. They'll settle for yesterday, but not 15 years ago. In fact, most employers do not keep records past seven years, and few check references beyond the three most recent employers. Capitalize on this knowledge to save valuable space and create a relevant resume.

If you have a large number of jobs from an earlier era, summarize with a statement like, "1950–60: Sales representative for several major fastener manufacturers."

This is the best practice for resume relevance, and you will probably learn more about yourself in the process. It's great preparation for your interview, too.

12. Be consistent in how you list.

Either title, then company name—or company name then title—is appropriate. Choose whichever you believe to be more noteworthy. Just be sure all listings are organized the same way. Don't waste space on complete company addresses. City and state are sufficient, if address is given at all.

13. Watch out for "time in job" problems.

Some occupations are expected to have more longevity than others. Generally, sales, marketing, and creative services people are expected to "job hop" more frequently than accountants and similar professionals.

Be aware of the average longevity in your field, as well as in target positions with employers. If your resume indicates a problem that might get you "screened out" instead of a screen test, combine positions. Instead of listing three consecutive two-year jobs as an engineering manager, write:

1980–86 Engineering Manager, Coating Technologies
    Industry

14. List education last.

A brief mention of educational credentials, *without* mentioning the dates degrees were received, should be the last item on the page.

This is sufficient:

M.S., Electrical Engineering, Drexel University
B.S., Electrical Engineering, Lehigh University

15. Keep it concise.

Avoid elaborate, multisyllabic words in compound sentences. Instead use a brief, simple presentation that will incite the interviewer to positive action—an invitation for an interview.

16.   Avoid "I-ing" the reader.

Leave the personal pronoun out altogether.

17.   Begin sentences with strong *action* words that signal your effectiveness:

"Developed a series of . . ."

"Organized a task force to . . ."

"Consistently performed . . ."

"Led a team investigating . . ."

"Managed and controlled a program to . . ."

Here are the most effective action verbs:

Accelerated	Certified
Achieved	Charted
Accomplished	Communicated
Administered	Compiled
Analyzed	Completed
Applied	Composed
Appointed	Conceived
Arbitrated	Conducted
Arranged	Concluded
Attained	Constructed
Audited	Consulted
Averted	Contracted
Budgeted	Controlled
Built	Converted
Calculated	Convinced

Counseled
Cut
Created
Decentralized
Decided
Delivered
Demonstrated
Designed
Detected
Determined
Developed
Devised
Diagnosed
Directed
Discovered
Dispensed
Doubled
Drafted
Edited
Eliminated
Established
Evaluated
Executed
Exhibited
Expanded
Expedited
Facilitated
Forecasted
Formulated
Founded
Generated
Guided
Handled

Headed
Identified
Implemented
Improved
Increased
Influenced
Initiated
Innovated
Installed
Instituted
Instructed
Introduced
Invented
Judged
Justified
Launched
Led
Maintained
Managed
Marketed
Maximized
Measured
Mediated
Modernized
Monitored
Motivated
Negotiated
Obtained
Operated
Ordered
Organized
Oversaw
Packaged

Participated

Performed

Pioneered

Planned

Prepared

Presented

Processed

Procured

Produced

Programmed

Promoted

Projected

Provided

Publicized

Published

Purchased

Raised

Recommended

Recruited

Reduced

Referred

Regulated

Renegotiated

Reorganized

Reported

Represented

Researched

Resolved

Responded

Restored

Revamped

Revitalized

Routed

Selected

Served

Set up

Simplified

Sold

Solved

Specified

Staffed

Standardized

Streamlined

Strengthened

Studied

Succeeded

Summarized

Supervised

Supported

Synthesized

Systematized

Taught

Tested

Traded

Trained

Translated

Traveled

Trimmed

Tripled

Uncovered

Undertook

Unified

United

Unraveled

Upgraded

Used

Utilized	Won
Verified	Worked
Weighed	Wrote
Widened	

18. Use your wonderful one page wisely.

Avoid repetition. If you did similar tasks in two or three different jobs, detail only the most recent positions.

Don't include information that is implied. (If you're listing college degrees there's no need to add that you have a high school diploma.)

Don't take up space with company addresses and phone numbers. You can supply them later.

19. Emphasize *results*, not responsibilities.

Don't just say you were a salesperson in a certain territory. Indicate that sales increased 50 percent over the previous year, that you were consistently 10 percent over objective, and so on.

If your efforts resulted in substantial savings, if you controlled a large budget, use those numbers to establish your credibility and your level of experience. Wherever possible, *quantify* outcomes that objectify your effectiveness.

20. Avoid abbreviations.

You can abbreviate the months of the year in the work experience section, or use "B.A." instead of "Bachelor of Arts" in the education section. Beyond that, acronyms and abbreviations do not enhance a resume and can confuse the reader.

For the sake of space, identifying names of organizations by lettters is permissible after you have spelled out the name once.

21. Write deliberately, and edit.

A good resume takes time. It should be written with careful thought and attention to detail. It should be reread and critiqued—by you and another—before it is produced in final form. Remember, no second chances. You have to get it right the first time.

CREATING THE STYLE

22.   Use the power of white space.

Don't crowd the page. White space helps important points stand out and makes the resume easier to read. Use one- or two-line phrases preceded by bullets instead of large blocks of type.

23.   Have your resume typeset in type no smaller than 10-point size.

Although typewritten resumes (in at least 12-pitch type) are acceptable, typeset resumes have become the standard for most managerial and executive positions.

Jobgetting typefaces are the more conservative styles, such as Times Roman, Century Schoolbook, and Palatino. These are readable, available, and acceptable. They are all serif types (see resume samples), which are considered to be traditional and businesslike. If your activity allows more latitude of expression (graphic artist, designer, architect, performing artist, etc.), Optima is a readable, contemporary sans-serif type you might select.

With a good desktop publishing service, your resume can have that typeset look for less than most traditional typesetters charge. Just be sure to proofread carefully, and make corrections. It's your image.

24. Use boldface and italic type sparingly.

The point of using these techniques is to *emphasize* something specific. Do not use italics or bold type on every other line. It's like shouting. It loses impact when done constantly.

25. If typewritten, make sure it's perfect.

The most effective typeface is Courier. The typing should be professional and error-free. Your resume should be typed on an electric or electronic typewriter (even printed on a letter-quality computer printer) with a carbon, not a cloth, ribbon. No erasures, white-outs, or smudges. If you don't have a good quality electric typewriter, hire a typing service. But, if you're going to that trouble, refer to Tips 23 and and 24.

26. Print in black ink on *quality* white paper.

Ivory stock can also be used, and the weight should be at least 24 pound. Gray is acceptable, but it is often difficult to read and photocopy. Any other ink or paper colors are a mistake. Your relationship with the interviewer is still too fragile, and your resume may receive attention for a negative reason. Save your individualism for your opening-night celebration.

27. Leave at least a one-inch border all around.

This is primarily for esthetic reasons, but it is customary for interviewers to write comments in the margins. If they have to attach another sheet, many will just move on to the next resume.

28. Center your name, address, and telephone number at the top.

If you move or change telephone numbers, prepare another resume. Never strike out, x-out, white out, print over, scratch out, or otherwise ruin your resume with a typewriter or writing instrument before sending it to a prospective employer.

29. If space allows, include a few choice items of personal data *at the bottom.*

Emphasize credentials and career-related affiliations. Age, height, weight, and marital status are not expected or necessary.

30. Do not use all capital letters.

Except for the word RESUME at the top (if you want to include it), avoid all capital letters in a word or a phrase. Boldface and italics, carefully used, provide all the necessary emphasis and are easier to read than capital letters.

MAJOR "DON'TS"

31. Don't update or emphasize in handwriting.

Update only by revising your entire resume, or attach an application form neatly typed in advance. Italic and boldface emphasis should be done at the time the resume is prepared, or not at all. The resume is *you* before they meet you in person. Make sure it has class.

32. Don't include names of references.

Instead, add a line at the bottom that reads, "Personal and professional references furnished upon request." References are too precious to annoy, and you want to be able to contact them *first* and give them the scoop on the specific job and employer.

There's an exception for highly motivated references within the target company. If you're relying on the endorsement of a current employee to get you in the door, make sure that person knows what you're doing before listing his or her name. Even so, it's better to refer to your reference in a cover letter. I covered this subject in detail in *The Perfect Job Reference*.[2]

33. Don't state a salary.

This goes for past earnings as well as what you'd like to be earning in a new job. At the early stages of the job search, it is a no-win gamble. Invariably, it will be too high or too low. Besides, your value to someone else or even to yourself is irrelevant. It should even be illegal to ask—an unnecessary invasion of privacy. All ads say, "Send resume and salary requirements." Ignore the latter.

34. Don't state your objective.

Unless you know it is the job being offered and you don't want to be considered for any other position. Your resume might qualify you for a much better position than you originally thought. And it likely qualifies you for others, as well.

Don't foreclose your options. Your objective is getting an interview.

35. Don't give a reason for leaving previous jobs.

That type of explanation is best left for the interview.

36. Don't include a photograph.

Unless you think you should be hired on your physical appearance alone. Consideration of your face in the hiring process violates federal, state, and local equal employment opportunity laws, except under very limited circumstances. My *personal* opinion is that you shouldn't. My *personnel* opinion is that you shouldn't. My *legal* opinion is that you can. But staff interviewers in some companies will not forward a resume with a photograph attached.

If you're really good looking, attaching a photo to your resume might get you a date. I seriously doubt it will get you a job.

37. Don't apologize for self-perceived "weaknesses."

If you don't have a college degree or all the qualifications advertised, never apologize or sound defensive in any employment communication. This includes resumes and cover letters. Accentuate the positive, even if you can't eliminate the negative. Do it well, and your audience will forget what you were supposed to have. (They never really knew in the first place!)

38. Don't editorialize.

Save the adjectives for your reviewers to use. Report the facts, don't make claims. "Won three national writing awards for technical articles" makes your point much more concisely and objectively than "exceptional writing skills."

39. Don't overuse "buzzwords."

Unless you're sure your audience will be impressed favorably, use vocabulary that can be understood by a varied audience. You should appear intelligent, qualified, and direct. "Buzzwords" are "*fuzz* words" to people outside your field. They reject what they don't understand because they don't want to show their ignorance by asking someone else.

40. Don't reveal your age or race.

Avoid inviting age discrimination by stating your age or date of birth. It isn't necessary to give dates you received college degrees.

Also avoid any direct or indirect reference to race. A seasoned personneler knows the racially dominated colleges, majors, and associations. You may be proud, but they may be prejudiced.

41. Don't mention firings or layoffs.

Although "merger mania" and "acquisition anarchy" have affected nearly every industry and put even the best out of work in recent years, there's still a strong stigma attached to "involuntary termination" and "layoff." So don't mention them in the resume. Writing that you left "voluntarily" even looks suspicious. Everyone knows how that works.

42. Don't be sarcastic, humorous, or patronizing.

It might get your resume noticed for the wrong reason. Let your background speak for itself—articulately, objectively, and professionally.

43. Don't use gimmicks to get attention.

The best gimmick I ever saw was a resume photoreduced and inserted into a fortune cookie. I took it to a personnel manager's meeting and was a big hit. Of course, it was an unfortunate fortune. The applicant didn't get the job. He's probably still on the loose.

You're trying to get your foot in the door, not your face on the floor.

44. Don't exaggerate or mislead.

The average classified advertisement draws 200 resumes. While that may lead you to believe your facts won't be checked, be careful. Since human resourcers are so overworked, certain facts will be checked routinely because they are easy to verify.

College degrees are among the facts that can be verified. If you left college just three units short of a degree, don't say you earned it. Rather, the education section of your resume should read:

University of Nevada; 4 years of undergraduate study in business administration

or

Drake University School of Law; 2 years

Exaggerations in the experience portion of your resume can also be easily checked. If they don't check out, you'll be checked off the list.

45. Don't send your resume with a cover letter.

A cover letter to an unidentified target can point you away from a position that's right for you. Unless you *really* know something about the job, or want to name the source of your referral, resist the temptation. Those overworked personnel people will think of it as just one more piece of paper to shuffle. Worse yet, they may never look past it to your resume.

Of course, if you are aiming at a departmental *decision maker*, an eye-catching cover letter has exactly the opposite effect. It directs you right where you want to be.

A well-written cover letter is crucial in this case. It serves to introduce you and interest a decision maker. If you've done your homework, this is the time to show what you know. (More on cover letters in *Jeff Allen's Best: Get the Interview.*[3]

46. Don't send your resume in response to "blind box" ads that don't reveal the employer's identity.

Companies are known to advertise just to scout the market for talent. You could be sending your resume to your own employer! I call it a "rubber resume"—and it lands in some very embarrassing places. Send a resume only when the company is clearly identified.

47. Don't use a resume-writing service.

Writing your own resume is an exercise you *must* do to prepare yourself for an effective job search. Discipline yourself to go through your past and select only that which truly matters. Then sit down and write copy that sells. It's the best practice for the rest of the search.

Resume services make everyone's background the same, package them the same, and even send them to the same employers! Some get opened—then get yawns. Only you can tell your own story the way it should be told.

Exceptional candidates have exceptional resumes—or is it the other way around?

MAJOR "DO'S"

48. Get a name for the envelope.

Make a telephone call (or several, if necessary) to get the name of an individual in the human resources department who is hiring for this position. An envelope with a name will get opened first.

49. If advantageous, bypass human resources completely.

If you know your industry well enough, you should be able to make a few phone calls to get the name of the supervisor who wrote the job requisition ("rec"). Send your resume to that person instead of the human resourcer. Even if he or she sends it back to human resources for screening, you will increase your chances of being remembered for an interview.

50. Consult an expert on grammar, spelling, and punctuation.

If you don't really know English usage, *pay* someone to copyedit and proofread your resume. Typing services are unreliable in this area. Some know what they are doing, many do not.

If you don't know an editor or an English teacher, call a local college and ask for the English department. Locate a faculty member to review the resume for a nominal fee.

Don't let the expert revoke your literary license, though. You're not writing for an essay contest—you're moving a product. You're marketing to sell those goods to the highest bidder. We offer you proven techniques that work.

51. Emphasize individual accomplishments.

Don't diffuse the spotlight with what the company or department accomplished—shine it on your role and the results you effected.

THINK MARKETING!

52. Have an objective.

Although in Tip 34 I told you not to write your objective on your resume, it's important to *have* an objective to write a good one. The more specific, the better. Then the qualifications you include in your resume will be focused toward that objective. With no stated objective, you're not likely to be screened out.

Your unwritten objective should include the position title, its responsibilities, its potential, the industry, the salary, and the region where you want to live. With a clear objective in mind, your resume will subtly steer you in the direction you want to go. It gets you the right interviews and the best offers.

53. Think of the employer as a customer.

You're selling a product and service. The product is you, the services are yours. What does the customer want or need? How can you communicate how your product and service meet its particular wants or needs?

54. Stress performance, not qualifications.

Will you improve productivity? Increase profits? Cut costs?
Create new products? Develop new services?

Will you make the company a better place than before you
were hired? How? Employers hire people they think will do jobs
they think need to be done.

Qualified applicants are everywhere. But employers hire
performers. It's not what you've done that counts, it's what
you'll do with what you've done.

55. Don't appear overqualified.

Too many statistics can be as negative as too few.

People who are overqualified are *disqualified*. Employers
know they will leave as soon as something better comes along.
They're right.

Talk about what you'll do for them—performance.

THINK STRATEGY

56. Time the arrival of the resume for the most attention.

If your resume arrives in Monday's mail, it has to compete with the Friday backlog and weekend delivery. If it arrives on a Friday, it could get ignored. Friday is notorious in personnel offices—terminations and exit interviews dominate the day.

Your resume should arrive on a Tuesday, Wednesday, or Thursday. If mailing within the local area, drop it in the mail on Monday morning. If to a more distant place, mail it on Friday for Tuesday delivery.

57. Use overnight delivery services in special cases.

If you're responding to an ad with a resume, and you haven't spoken directly to the hirer, don't hyperventilate with overnight delivery. Nobody hires that fast, and you'll look too anxious.

However, if you've spoken directly to the hirer, your resume (with a brief, brilliant cover letter), arriving the next day via overnight express service, will have maximum impact. Your conversation will be remembered. Those "urgent" cardboard envelopes get delivered and opened immediately.

If you use this strategy, be sure to use a service that guarantees delivery by midmorning. Even overnight packages go through the mail room. Those arriving in the afternoon may not get to their destination until the next day.

Don't use your present employer's account or preprinted forms to send your resume in this manner. Besides tipping someone in your own mail room off to your secret search, it tells the target company that you are dishonest.

Instead, use one of the private mail service companies located near you. Stop in on your lunch hour and arrange and pay for the services yourself.

58. Follow up.

After going to such trouble to write the perfect resume and get it to the right person, don't just sit back and wait for the phone to ring or to find a "don't call us, we'll call you" form letter in your mailbox.

Keep a list of the resumes you sent, when you sent them, and to whom. Mark your calendar to call each individual within one week of the date your resume should have arrived, to confirm they received it. Make yourself known. But be polite, professional, and urgent. Try:

Them: Human Resources, Emma Waverly.

You: Good morning, Ms. Waverly. This is William Tucker. I sent you a resume last week for the position of _____, and I'm calling to verify that you've received it.

Them: Just a moment, Mr. Tucker. Let me check.

(This is also a good opportunity to learn the name of the person reviewing resumes for the position you want.)

> Yes, it's here. It is being reviewed by our professional development staff at this time.

You: I have to decide on an offer or keep looking, and I'd really like to talk to someone at Amalgamated before deciding. Could you give me the name of the (person in charge of reviewing resumes or hiring supervisor) so that I can call that individual and find out if I will be interviewed in the near future?

Them: Alright, Mr. Tucker. That would be Jim Farrell, Extension 2345. He's the department manager.

You: Thank you, Ms. Waverly.

It might not go so well in every instance. Your request could be met with a verbal version of "don't call us, we'll call you." In that case, thank the person as politely as possible. At least you have connected a pleasant personality to your name. If you push too hard, your resume could land in the wastebasket in retaliation. Hirers hold all the cards.

Chapter

2

Resumes for Specific Professions

Resume Tips 1 through 58 in Chapter 1 apply to all jobseekers, regardless of profession or rank. They're general rules for all good resumes. Now let's get specific, with resume tips for specific professions and situations.

The resume of a senior executive or middle manager will be different from that of someone at an entry level. Resumes for technical types, such as engineers and scientists, are different, too.

EXECUTIVE AND PROFESSIONAL RESUMES

Senior executives, middle managers, and professionals are all judged rigorously by prospective employers. If you're one of them, your resume must be exceptional. Otherwise, you won't get a chance to show what you know at the screen test—the interview.

You've undoubtedly learned to develop a successful business plan. Now you must develop your career plan. The discipline that helped you succeed in your work will help here, as well.

Besides facing a more rigorous set of standards, executives, managers, and professionals are up against more competition than ever. Loretta D. Foxman writes in *The Executive Resume Book*:

> It is estimated that more than 100,000 upper-level and mid-level management and executive positions were eliminated by downsizing, mergers, and acquisitions in the late 1980s, and there seems to be no relief in sight. The executive who has a job today may be out of work tomorrow through no fault of his or her own.[4]

Many executives fail to bring the competitive edge to their job search that they bring to their job. On the job, they concentrate their talent and skill on formulating a strategy that meets the realities of business. But few executives faced with making a career move bring their talent and skill to creating the right resume and developing a strategy to get it noticed.

I've encountered many $100,000+-a-year executives who say, "I'm starting on this search right now. I don't want to waste time on a new resume. I'll just update my current one."

"Current" probably means at least five years old. The world changes in five years, and people with it. These same executives would never settle for resurrecting a five-year old business plan to meet their companies' future requirements.

Although *action* and *achievement* have promoted executives to where they are, taking the time to strategize is an essential part of a successful search. It may take a week to get the resume right, but it's a week well spent. *Not* taking the time to do it right could easily mean months of rejection—and years of "rejection shock" that can knock any jobseeker cold.

59. Set your goal—and organize to achieve it.

Goal-setting is important in any career plan. However, it takes on even greater significance in the executive job search. Your resume should reflect your ability to define a goal, develop a strategy to achieve it, and succeed. That's why you're called an "executive"—you *execute*. You get things done.

Your objective should include:

- The name of the position.
- The responsibilities and potential.
- The type of company and industry.
- The company size.

- Who you will report to.
- What you will report.
- The salary you will receive.

Include the area of the country you prefer and what office environment is important to you.

Write down your objective in one or two concise sentences. This is for you alone. Your resume won't state an objective, but practically everything on the resume should be aimed toward it.

Memorize that one- or two-sentence objective. Tape it to your mirror and on that carving board that pulls out on your desk. Slip it into your wallet near your credit cards. You gotta have a dream if you're gonna make a dream come true.

60. Put yourself in the prospective employer's place.

Knowing what *you* want is half the job. Knowing what employers want is the other half. You have to scope out your target companies and learn how they operate, what they value, and what they think needs to be done.

A resume should answer the questions employers ask. In the case of executives, these questions increase in scope. Make sure your resume states:

- How you can increase productivity.
- How you can improve profits.
- How you can enhance services.
- Items that demonstrate your ability to perform.
- That you know the employer's business.

- That you understand the customers' needs.
- How you can make the hirer look good.

Once you've targeted the jobs that meet *your* objectives, your resume is likely to meet the employer's. They're always there in the background—setting the stage.

61. Adopt a market-driven approach.

Match what you have to offer to what is needed today. Look for a job that no longer exists and that is exactly what you'll get.

On the way up the ladder, you've had to sell yourself: your ideas, goals, and approaches. You've been playing to your audience—servicing your employer's needs. Your action has been specific and results-oriented. It worked, too.

The same techniques must be employed in positioning yourself for a better career.

Sell the features (qualifications) and benefits (performance) of the *product* (you) and *services* (yours). Companies don't buy executives—they buy a stronger bottom line, a more effective marketing program, solutions to their problems. *Know* the problems they face and *show* how you can solve them.

62. Reveal only what the employer needs and wants to know.

Don't include information that's unrelated to your career objective. If you have had a long career, emphasize the most applicable, current, impressive accomplishments.

63. Mention outside activities if they help.

Include outside activities if they demonstrate your value to the company and skills you will use in your work. An example might be management and leadership of a successful fund-raising campaign. When listing church activities, you should omit a religious affiliation to minimize possible discrimination. Since you're an executive, you should know better than to include one anyway.

List military experience (including accomplishments) if you were an officer. If you enlisted or were noncommissioned, mention it only to explain a gap in employment.

64. Know who will be reviewing your resume.

Executive-level jobseekers are often advised to direct their resumes to the highest appropriate official—CEO, CFO, COO, president, managing partner, or senior vice-president. But recent studies[5] suggest that executives at this level do not screen unsolicited resumes.

Two-thirds of unsolicited resumes for executive-level positions received by senior officials are delegated for screening to employees at the director or manager level—usually in the human resources department.

That knowledge is helpful since you were a director or manager. You know how they think, what they've been told is important, and what they look for in a resume.

When recommending a candidate to his or her superior, a manager or director will be sure the resume matches the job requisition ("rec") and the corporate culture. So, if you know the target company has a reputation for only hiring executives with certain credentials (like an M.B.A. from one of the major business schools) be ready. If you don't have that credential, counterbalance the negative with a positive (the dean's list, a scholastic award, etc.).

If you're going to send an unsolicited resume, design it to be first in line at the casting call. Know what a manager or director is conditioned to spot, and make sure it's there.

65. Don't use unusual formats.

Every size, shape, and smell of resume lands on a hiring desk. I used to tell people I was a pilot. I'd "pile it" here, then I'd "pile it" there. Miles and miles of piles and files.

And eventually they'd fall into that great final file on the floor.

Once you've focused on your objective and developed your strategy for achieving it, you won't need to get attention for the wrong reason. Your ability will speak for itself.

Your resume should be first class. Professional, understated, and direct. Like you.

66. Polish your resume to perfection.

According to a survey of hiring officials and recruiters conducted by Loretta Foxman, the most important factor in a resume is "neatness."

You have been told that neatness counts ever since you first learned to write. When you consider that your resume can affect the rest of your life, you can begin to understand the importance of the way it looks. If it looks inviting to read, it will be read, even if the recruiter is overworked and it's 11:00 P.M. A neat resume says, "Look at me. I'm easy to read. I won't take much of your time."[6]

Besides neatness, typesetting and white space were also cited as important factors. Predictably, sloppiness, typographical errors, misspellings, and incorrect grammar were all rejection reasons.

67. Include dates.

Stick to the chronological format. When hiring "big-ticket" managers, companies are especially careful to check exact dates of education and employment. They want to know what you've done recently, so emphasize current achievements.

68. Mention unusual experiences only if they'll drive up your value.

Self-employment, or personal time off for "self-discovery," can work for or against you.

It's better to downplay the yearlong vacation you took to sail around the world. Employers will think you'll do it again. It's also evidence of individualism that runs contrary to "team spirit."

But two years in the Peace Corps might have taught you skill and insight useful to an employer. So would a yearlong executive management program at a business school.

Consulting between corporate assignments also can be received favorably, if presented in the right way. Be prepared for the question, "If you were successfully self-employed, why did you return to a job?" You can explain that a company pursued you and made you an offer to run it you couldn't refuse. Perhaps you can explain that you preferred being a player instead of a coach.

If you started consulting, then gave up when it didn't work out, better not mention it.

---

69. Begin with a "power summary."

This initial statement on an executive's resume will usually determine whether it gets on the "to be interviewed" pile. Use action language, quantifiable results, and a direct style to summarize properly.

Not this:

As the Public Relations Director for a large West Coast corporation, I have top-level corporate experience with heavy staff advisory, policy-building, and administrative responsibility; excellent writing and speaking skills and strong editorial background are other attributes.

But this:

Director of Public Relations for Fortune 500 financial service corporation. Controlled budget of $5.6 million and staff of 40. Established media buying policy and revitalized corporate image.

Let's see what's wrong with the first summary. It should be evident. It's "flat" and rambles. It talks about "experience" and "responsibility" without focusing on accomplishments. It lacks numbers to tell the reader a level of experience. What does "large West Coast corporation" mean?

Further, what does "strong editorial background" mean? That he or she has been slaving away at the word processor writing the copy for press releases? That's not top management work.

The first summary lacks the positive action words that appear in the second: "Directed," "controlled," "established," "revitalized." The second clearly communicates the candidate's level of experience, with the designation "Fortune 500," and by stating the size of budget and staff control. The word "revitalized" suggests a turnaround that could interest the reader in the candidate.

That's the purpose of the power summary—to hit the reader between the eyes with words that motivate and activate him or her to call you.

Refer to the list of action words that follows Tip 17 for valuable additions to your power vocabulary.

70. Follow your power summary with tangible achievements.

Employers don't want to know what you attempted or what you were supposed to do. They want to know what you achieved. They want to know the benefits that directly resulted from your decisions.

71. Give a short synopsis of previous employers' statistics.

Whenever a current or former employer's size, sales volume,

market share, or industry dominance can lend credibility to your credentials, make this information known.

 Edit and critique.

Your resume should be edited at least three times. On the first pass, eliminate unnecessary words, clarify ambiguous phrases, and generally tighten up the statements.

Not "responsible for," but "directed, "managed," "controlled." *Never* "coordinated." (Top managers don't coordinate.)

On the second pass, *eliminate* the unnecessary and *illuminate* the essential. Emphasize the areas that make you most valuable to a prospective employer. No matter how much you cherish that award from 20 years ago, don't mention it unless it can help you now. Use every syllable to your best advantage.

Finally, proofread for spelling, grammar, and punctuation. Make sure your punctuation is consistent. Give your resume to two other knowledgeable people to proofread.

Then, critique your resume carefully and have others you trust critique it as well.

---

73. Test market.

As a final test of your completed resume, make 10 copies of your final draft and distribute them to your "network"—trusted friends and colleagues with exposure to top management. Ask for their honest evaluation of the resume's impact, clarity, and appeal.

Put your finished resume aside for one or two days before sending it out. Reread it again to make sure it profiles you properly.

RESUMES FOR SCIENCE AND ENGINEERING PROFESSIONS

Although all the general resume rules apply to scientists and engineers, there are distinctions. Minor deviations in format, tone, and length are acceptable. I'll discuss such exceptions here.

Scientists and engineers are also excused from omitting insider vocabulary. It is necessary for those with technical backgrounds to use language and abbreviations commonly understood by other technical types. If they didn't, it would be impossible to limit the resume to one page.

Their resumes should still be one page long, arranged in chronological format. The career summary is followed by professional experience, then education (the most current position or degree first). It should omit personal data and names of references, and follow all the rules of form and substance already mentioned. Exceptions and variations follow.

74. Packing punch into the career summary.

If you were responsible for an invention, discovery, patent, or other innovation that contributed to your field or employer, highlight it in your career summary rather than at the bottom under "Publications, Honors, and Awards." Showcasing such important data early will attract attention.

Of course, make sure its value is mentioned.

75. When education comes first.

Scientists and engineers with incredible educational credentials can put their education before their work experience. It establishes qualifications, particularly in the case of advanced degrees from leading universities.

List the degree awarded (abbreviation is fine), followed by the institution. Date awarded is not necessary. In most cases, it isn't necessary to give an address for the college. If you do, include only the city and state.

Recent graduates can cover educational experience in more detail, since it's what they have to offer. Follow the listing of degrees, institutions, and dates with a chronological (last first) summary of important studies, projects, papers published, etc.

76. Summarize professional accomplishments in reverse chronological order.

Again, the general rules apply. Use the power vocabulary and short phrases instead of long sentences. Science and engineering resumes lend themselves to bulleted lists under each employer name and job title. It helps the reader focus on the technical data given.

77. List certificates, licenses, and clearances.

Special certificates and licenses, along with government clearances for classified work, should appear prominently.

78. Include publications, honors, and awards.

Accolades received, papers presented at professional meetings, symposium proceedings published, articles in recognized journals, and anything else for which a scientist has received recognition are especially meaningful in the job search. However, too many resumes of technical jobseekers dribble like doctoral dissertations.

Up to a full page of highlights—*as an attachment* to a one-page resume—is acceptable. A prolific Ph.D. can mention his or her work with a notation at the bottom of his or her one-page resume that reads: "Publications and Awards—See Addendum." If incomplete, the listing can end with the words, "Partial list only. Complete list of publications furnished upon request."

79. Mention professional affiliations and positions, if space permits.

If there's still room, include memberships in professional societies, and note past or current offices.

80. Highlight foreign languages and special skills.

The ability to speak other languages is exceptionally important when targeting multinational employers. Use your judgment.

81. Exceptions to the one-page rule.

With everything an experienced scientist or engineer could pack into a resume, early drafts usually exceed one page. Once you've written it, look closely at all the information you've included and determine what might be cut to reduce it to one page: one attractive, comfortably spaced page, not one scientific formula containing your development from an embryo.

If you edit and re-edit and still exceed one page, don't sell your sliderule. It's okay—it's just not recommended. Resumes are reviewed by someone who screens within a minute or so. The chance of your being invited for an interview diminishes by *20 percent* for every page. That's one scientific fact I hope you don't prove.

Chapter

3

Special Problems

Chapter 1 gave you 58 general rules to follow to prepare a super resume. Chapter 2 added special rules for senior managers, top executives, scientists, and engineers.

But because every individual is unique, almost everyone encounters some "special problem" in conforming his or her resume to these guidelines. Very few candidates graduated from college, then earned an advanced degree at the "right" age, then rose up the ranks at all the "right" companies with promotions at all the "right" intervals.

This section addresses those special problems jobseekers encounter in writing a resume that gets results. Dealing with layoffs, midlife job changes, initially entering the workforce, reentering it, or changing careers presents special challenges. All these obstacles can be overcome if you know how.

Your resume is your 8 x 10 glossy. It gets you the invitation to audition. You can't risk something in your resume disqualifying you before you deliver your lines. So read on . . .

82. The downsized jobseeker.

I wrote my book *Surviving Corporate Downsizing*[7] to help employees stay and suceed during the chaos of corporate contractions. The techniques I presented were geared to ensuring job security while identifying and maximizing the incredible opportunities a downsize presents.

If you've been downsized out and are still trying to get back in where you belong, here's how your resume can help:

In spite of the fact that hundreds of thousands of qualified people were downsized during the last decade, termination or layoff implications in a resume are job-busters. If you've been laid off—or are about to be—don't apologize for it, explain it, or include it in anyway. Your explanations are best given in the interview, when you've already had a chance to meet personally and rehearse your response. For now, you don't owe total strangers any explanation.

If you're currently unemployed as a result of a downsize, you could easily be down on yourself, too. You *shouldn't* be, but it's normal. The process of writing your resume, of reviewing a career of turning obstacles into opportunities, should give you a needed review of reality. It's hard not to feel like a victim, but you mustn't or you'll end up with a can instead of a career.

Accentuate the positive. Proudly list your achievements. Write a dynamite list of credits to the rerun of your life.

If you've been told you're on the way out, or the locks have just been changed on your office door, get a copy of *Surviving Corporate Downsizing* and read it. I review every possible way to make a job transition while you're still employed.

One of the most important things you can do right now is secure a good reference. Use your employer's guilt about letting you go. Present management with your arsenal of facts, including positive performance reviews and lists of accomplishments. Show them you were an asset.

Write a reference and get management's approval. Have your supervisor write a letter of reference from it. In many states, once they've said something favorable, they can't change their mind without notifying you and justifying it. (In *The Perfect Job Reference*[8], I cover this topic in detail.) You can concentrate on your career without the noise of any rattling skeletons.

If you're unemployed and jobseeking during the same calendar year in which you were terminated, your resume can read:

1987–90 Materials Manager, American Southwest Corporation

It's a little harder to disguise a downsize if you're looking the following year. But it's not impossible. You just have to prepare the power summary and accomplishments carefully to keep potential employers' attention on you rather than the dates.

83. The midlife resume

The 64 million baby boomers born from 1946 to 1964 have affected American life wherever they've gone. When they were youngsters, we built more elementary schools to teach them. When they grew up, colleges expanded to meet their needs. In the 1970s, when college educated boomers hit the workforce, everyone wanted to be young. Old was out. Youth was favored over wisdom.

But the youthful boomers are getting older and wiser. Forty doesn't look so old anymore. Now it's fashionable to be 40—even 50—as more and more people are.

America's population is aging, and older workers will enjoy more acceptance and respect in the 1990s than they did in the 1970s and 1980s. So, don't worry about changing jobs over 40. You've got a lot of good years ahead of you. As I wrote in *Finding the Right Job at Midlife*:

> There's never been a better time for finding a job at midlife. . . . Technology has created a service-oriented economy with the number of jobs increasing faster than the number of applicants. . . .

Your success in . . . changing jobs after the age of 40 really comes down to just three things:

1. Developing the right attitude about your abilities.
2. Organizing an effective job campaign; and
3. Overcoming the myths in our society about midlife employees.[9]

Although the 1990s may very well become the decade when 40 is fashionable and 50 is fine, it's best to recognize that age prejudice remains. Don't advertise your age. Instead, sort through the depth of your life experience to reveal *only* the accomplishments that demonstrate how you qualify for the target job.

Don't make typical midlife mistakes: a resume that states an objective, indicates that children are grown, rambles about job functions (not achievements), runs on for more than one page, and is prepared by a resume service. You'll get responses to these—rejection letters.

A properly drafted midlife resume can be indispensable to *ensure* an interview. Go through the job inventory process described in Chapter 1. For each former job, list the highest achievement *related to the job you seek*, then continue with less relevant items. When you run out of space, go back and cut from the bottom on each position.

Combine or omit short-term employment. Don't list everything you've done, or even every place you've done it. You're not applying for security clearance, you're just applying for a job!

You're in the unique position of being able to show what you want potential employers to know. Your resume will be an album of your "greatest hits"—all on one side of one record.

Don't list dates you received college degrees or other educational credentials. (If you earned your degrees through continuing education while employed, you can appear younger. If you think it will help, fine.)

Then prepare your approach to answering the phone. You'll be receiving calls from interested employers soon.

Oh, you never knew that they *called*? They do—when they're *really* interested. Why? Your resume presold them!

---

84. The reentry resume.

"Reentry" is a word usually followed by "woman." Women are told by checkstand articles and daytime talk show guests that years as a personal agent, household manager, financial manager, child-care provider, community volunteer—and a dozen other unpaid job titles—amount to valuable, maybe even rewarding, experience.

It's true. You have skills and experience far beyond a paycheck player. You've subordinated your dreams to your family. That demonstrates the ultimate in self-discipline and compassion. After working 16-hour days for the past 10 or 20 years, a "full-time job" will seem like a vacation.

Unfortunately, people who screen your resume don't award "work experience" credits for all you've done. So write a reentry resume that emphasizes your ability, skill, and accomplishments.

Here are some of the accomplishments from the resume of a midlife woman with four children, recently divorced, lacking any paid work experience, but active in volunteer work:

1980 to present: **Director,**
                         National Youth Assistance
                               Organization,
                         Los Angeles, California

1. Implemented a complete system of reporting between chapters to improve communication and maximize use of equipment.

2. Supervised a field staff responsible for conducting local and regional projects.

3. Led a successful drive to reestablish necessary dialogue with civic and business leaders.

4. Motivated the directors of other chapters to devise new ways to obtain contributions from sponsors.

1976 to 1980   Administrator
Community Improvement Program
Santa Monica, California

1. Initiated the preparation of an operations manual for use by inspectors.

2. Strengthened the existing public relations activities, including interface with media-buying service.

3. Prepared reports for city and state agencies to ensure their continued support.

4. Streamlined internal paper flow so that the efforts of staff workers would be maximized.[10]

If you've served in any volunteer capacity—PTA officer, nursery school board of directors, city commission, election campaign—you've got management, leadership, and organizational experience that can directly apply to the target job.

If you don't have volunteer experience, thoroughly evaluate what you like to do, what you do best (usually what you like), and what you want to be doing (usually what you've liked). Then check adult education and community college course offerings for skill drills and prepare to go in at an entry level—just temporarily. As I wrote in *Finding the Right Job at Midlife*:

> If you are entering the job market after a long absence, the best thing to do is jump right into *skills training*. An entry-level job is the optimum way, since you'll "earn while you learn." Classified advertisements, public and private placement offices, and "cold-calling" businesses that have jobs in the field—any jobs—are the places to start. If you can afford it, volunteer time in exchange for training can also be valuable. The only classes to consider are those that teach specific, marketable *skills* or have a "work component." Sitting somewhere listening to abstract theory may be fine for youngsters, but if you're not careful, midlife will pass you by. Employers want *skills*.[11]

Aim at companies that will reimburse tuition and books. Learn specific skills and your life experience will fuel your future.

85. The entry-level resume.

Recent college grads should highlight college achievements such as awards, honors, and class standing. Include internships, special projects, and part-time employment during high school and college to demonstrate your accomplishments. Results of studies you conducted, titles of papers you wrote (published or not), relating to your target field, will demonstrate your ability. Include a special section highlighting any volunteer or service work and offices held.

Chapter 5 contains samples of entry-level resumes. References from professors and influential friends will augment yours.

Even ask for help in setting up interviews. Use whatever contacts you can to get an audition.

The two other books in the *Jeff Allen's Best* series show you how to get hired when you're someone needing experience to get experience. *The Perfect Job Reference* outlines the way to form, increase, and benefit from your very own fan club.

Then you'll call your entry-level resume your "open sesame resume."

86. The change-of-occupation resume.

The working world is turning faster than ever. By the year 2000, it will be spinning. Discoveries and opportunities are creating new industries while antiquing others. At the same time, the average career life is increasing to 50 years. With these and other factors operating, changing occupations will become almost as common as changing jobs.

When targeting a position in a new field or industry, emphasize transferable skills. As I told readers in *Finding the Right Job at Midlife*:

> In conducting outplacement programs, I discovered that there is over 50 percent "job comparability" or similarity between all occupations, so far as the day-to-day work is concerned. However, if you "go for what you know," it can be much higher. . . .

> An important exercise is to write down the jobs related to your present one ("job family"), then those that require similar skills ("crossover jobs"). While the first

list may look like a combination of Scrabble™ and Trivial Pursuit™, reworking it a few times will start your mind creatively expanding the options. Although you may already be familiar with the job family, you can discover many crossover jobs by reading the *Dictionary of Occupational Titles*, annually published by the United States Department of Labor. It contains the names and brief descriptions of thousands of jobs, and is available at your public library reference desk.

There is a great difference between skills that are *actually* transferable and those that can be *marketed* as transferable. The employer doesn't know unless you emphasize the transferable skills. Therefore, it is often helpful to work *backward*, taking the job description and plugging in your applicable experience to the resume and dialogue. . . . [B]efore long you will be astounded at how closely your skills [and accomplishments] are aligned with the job you are seeking. [Y]our life experience just needs focusing. And marketing.[12]

Changing occupations takes more research than changing jobs. It's time spent wisely, because it will pay off with work you like at a salary you deserve.

Aim for target companies by doing research at your local library. Use your network to talk to people who work in those companies or at jobs you'd like to be doing. Learn all you can about the field and players. Then your resume will look like you've been an insider all along.

Avoid language and vocabulary specific to your present occupation. Whether you're in marketing, operations, or manufacturing, emphasize the skills and accomplishments usable in the new industry.

Your resume should demonstrate that you are a person with drive and intelligence that can compensate for your lack of specific experience. Show past accomplishments that prove you're a "quick study." Any previous career or responsibility change should indicate that the change was successful.

You have reason to be confident about a career change. In a study conducted of employers, Loretta Foxman learned that "not even half of those surveyed (45 percent)" thought industry experience was essential in getting hired. Another 23 percent said it's "nice to have" and 32 percent believed it did not matter. Following are some quotes from employers responding to Foxman's survey:

> "Related experience or direct experience helps . . . but they [candidates] must show proven track record in anything they've done."

> "[Experience is] important for a technical or scientific position; otherwise, it varies according to the job."

> "[S]ignificant experience in other industries sharing common characteristics . . . is necessary.[13]

87. Too many jobs?

Foxman's survey also asked employers to give the optimum number of employers. Their answers were:

- 44 percent prefer "several"
- 40 percent prefer "one or two"
- 16 percent prefer "other "

Following are some of the comments from respondents to Foxman's survey:

"One (or two) employers demonstrates stability."

"Usually several [employers] . . . depends on level or amount of time with each."

"Someone who has only been with one company worries me."

"Experience and tenure more important than number [of employers]."

"Too much job hopping, particularly without a clearly evident career path, is a negative."

"Two to four, all related to core experience, gives broader experience."[14]

If you've changed jobs frequently, search among the accomplishments in your job inventory and pull out the ones that relate to a central theme, preferably directly related to the job you are seeking.

You could also try grouping jobs together, as in the functional resume. This would change the format of your resume from chronological to combination. Less than a year's tenure in more than one position is a siren that blasts "instability." You may have a good explanation, but you're not going to be giving it if your resume warns potential employers to get out of the way.

If your recent past has been more stable than the earlier years, eliminate the negative.

88. Too few jobs?

As Foxman's survey revealed in Tip 87, employers may worry if they see only one employer on your resume. Not a risk taker? Too security conscious? Why is he or she changing with so much time invested?

Avoid these impressions by creating a resume that shows diversity of responsibilities and accomplishments within that organization. Promotions to progressively higher levels and jobs in different areas that gave you diverse experience can be even more effective on a resume than employer changes. There's a direct value in conveying loyalty and stability.

If you have been at the same job for 10 or more years with no change in title, emphasize accomplishments, projects, and components of the job that developed your ability.

Chapter

4

Video Resumes

With the availability and lower cost of video technology, we're receiving more video resumes at the National Placement Law Center. You've probably noticed books and articles advocating them, and suggesting how they can be done.

I'm not aware of any cases where a video resume has enhanced a jobseeker's marketability. But I see many where one has destroyed it.

When you enter an interviewer's office, you're an actor taking a screen test. Before the greeting, you have a star's standard stage fright. But as soon as you smile and shake hands, the adrenalin subsides and you're giving a professional performance. You're interacting with the audience—and playing to it. The video camera gives very few jobseekers that advantage.

Legally, video resumes encourage *unequal* opportunity employers. They start having a negative reaction to affirmative action. Unlawful discrimination is the result. Race, height, weight, and age should not (and legally *cannot*) be considered in hiring someone. The exceptions to that law are so limited that you won't encounter them. You'll encounter discrimination, though. You just won't know it.

However, if you send a resume or present yourself by phone, a video can be legally used instead of an interview. It's still not going to get you hired, but if you must . . .

89. Don't do it yourself.

If you do, send it to ABC. You won't get hired, but you may see your face on *America's Funniest Home Videos*.

Professional videotape services are probably listed in your *Yellow Pages* under "Videotaping Studios," "Video Production Services," and similar headings.

90. Simulate an interview.

Use a service with an office set. It should look like an interview taking place in an interviewer's office.

You won't get hired this way either, but at least you'll look professional.

91. Avoid a production-line resume service.

Some services allow you to select different questions and sets. It's the equivalent of different paper and formats at a traditional resume service . . . with the same (lack of) results.

92. Prepare!

The preparation is the same as for a written resume. From there, you will need to "script" an interview with questions that encourage realistic answers to highlight your attributes.

93. Select a good off-camera interviewer.

Interacting with another (who is heard but not seen) is critical. The person you select as an off-camera interviewer will have to sound credible as well.

94. Rehearse.

Rehearse thoroughly with your "interviewer." Tape your rehearsals and critique your delivery. Check for awkward mannerisms, nervous gestures, unclear speech, and the like.

95. Dress the part.

Appear on camera as you would at an interview. For men, the jobgetting interview uniform consists of a dark blue suit, white shirt, conservative tie, and polished black leather shoes. For women, a conservative, dark-colored business suit with minimal makeup and jewelry is the jobgetting interview uniform. (More on preparing for the interview in *Jeff Allen's Best: Win the Job.*)

96. Keep it short.

Fifteen minutes is the longest your video should run. If you can get it into five, all the better. Your written resume gets only two minutes. Make sure you open in a way that grabs and holds the audience's attention.

97. Make copies.

Even if a few employers send them back, you'll probably be at retirement age. Buy as many copies as there are companies you'll be targeting. The more copies produced, the lower the unit price.

The video production company will gleefully quote prices for copies at the same time they tell you what the master copy will cost.

98. Announce your arrival.

Don't mass-mail video resumes. (Yes, it happens.) Call your target companies, get the name of someone in human resources (or the hiring supervisor), and let that person know you'll be visiting via video.

99. Send your written resume with your video.

All the written resume rules apply. A video resume should be accompanied by a copy of your written resume and a cover letter.

100. If all else fails, use your video to improve your interview performance.

Videotaping is a good way to prepare for an interview. Before you copy or send your video resume, preview it with your family or friends. Critique *yourself* honestly, too. If *you* wouldn't hire you based on what you see, then trash the tape, keep working on your interview style, and consider the expense your tuition to the College of Interview Knowledge.

Chapter

5

Sample Resumes

This chapter presents resumes from various professions. Some of the jobgetters represented are experienced; others are entry level. In each case, I'll show you the resume that was *used before* the jobgetter learned the resume techniques in this book. Following each resume are my comments and a revision based on my 100 tips for resumes that win.

ACCOUNTANT

Regrettable

Andrew M. Erikson
25 Hilltop Road
Birmingham, AL 35203

CAREER OBJECTIVE: To join a major corporation as
accountant and eventually become controller or
treasurer.   **1**

Education   **2**

Bachelor of Science, Accounting; University of
Alabama, 1983-1989

Attended college evenings while working full time in
controller's department of Gulfstream Enterprises and
Davis Aerospace Corporation.

Advanced Accounting Courses	Business Background Courses

Managerial Accounting
Accounting for Decision-making
COBOL I & II
Advanced Federal Taxation
Seminar in Management
  Accounting

Financial Management
Industrial Economics
Management
  Information Systems
Strategic Management

Experience   **3**

Staff Accountant, Gulfstream Enterprises, Huntsville,
Alabama, 1988 - present

Worked on various assignments in the Controller's
office using IBM ledger system. This related to
computer accounting training at the University of
Alabama and enabled me to accept increased

responsibility. Desire change because my degree
qualifies me **4** for advanced responsibility not
possible in present position. Discussed this decision
thoroughly with the Controller, who requested that I
remain with Gulfstream until I find a new position.

Accounting Supervisor, Davis Aerospace Corporation;
Birmingham, Alabama, 1983-1988.

Full-charge and general-ledger bookkeeping. Worked
with IBM ledger system, prepared financial
statements, and rotated as backup accounting clerk as
needed.

References **5**

Edward N. Albrough, Controller, Gulfstream
Enterprises; 34 River Avenue, Birmingham, Alabama
35204 (205) 999-4567

Howard Stone, Ph.D., Professor of Accounting,
University of Alabama, P.O. Box 345, Tuscaloosa,
Alabama 35401 (205) 654-3219

Comments

By the look of this resume, Andrew Erikson is new to resume writing, and followed bad advice. He's destined to be a staff accountant with his present employer for a long time unless he makes some major changes. Let's look at some of the problems.

1. **Tip 34, "Don't state an objective."**

   This one's even worse because it's ambiguous. "Oh, maybe I'll be controller, maybe treasurer, *eventually*." Indefinite goals, not well reasoned. Skip the objective and include a summary of achievements instead.

2. **Tip 14, "List education last."**

   New graduates without professional achievements but with excellent educational credentials are an exception to this rule. This jobseeker has relevant experience and accomplishments that should be presented first.

   Before we find out where he excels, we have to wade through practically his whole transcript of courses. He fails to even mention his *accomplishments* in school. He would have lost a resume screener by now.

   While it's commendable that he earned a degree while working full time in his field, he didn't mention whether his grades were above average. Most hirers know the curriculum for an accounting degree. If they're interested, they'll request a transcript *after* the initial interview. Using valuable upper space for a list of courses wastes a valuable opportunity.

3. **Tip 19, "Emphasize *results*, not responsibilities."**

Instead of using strong action words describing accomplishments, effectiveness, and results, this writer "worked on various assignments." "Worked with IBM ledger system." "Rotated as backup accounting clerk." Weak, unimpressive, and unclear as to his capability.

Before preparing his resume, this candidate did not inventory his six years' experience. As a result, he failed to enhance his resume with any examples of performance, results, or effectiveness.

4. **Tip 35, "Don't give a reason for leaving previous jobs."**

Not only does he give a reason, but he volunteers that his present employer wants him to keep right on working until he finds a new position. It doesn't contribute to understanding what kind of accountant this man is, and what he can contribute to a new employer.

5. **Tip 32, "Don't include names of references."**

Wasted space, better used to market himself as a proven performer. "References are too precious to annoy, and you want to be able to contact them *first* and give them the scoop on the specific job and employer."

General Comments

The language of this resume is weak. The sentences are too long, the vocabulary too loose. This candidate conveys low self-esteem. Otherwise (an amateur psychologist thinks), he might have presented himself in a more positive, persuasive manner.

It's unfortunate, because this fellow performed admirably at his last two jobs. He also earned high honors in college while working full time, studying only part time for his degree. The rewrite that follows turns this disoriented job*seeker* into a direct job*getter*.

In the revision, Andrew uses the power of white space, action words, and key phrases arranged in bulleted-list format. It shows what he knows and how successfully he can perform. We transformed his former typewritten pages into an effective type-set one with careful use of bold type.

Which Andrew Erikson would you hire?

Revised

Andrew M. Erikson
25 Hilltop Road
Birmingham, Alabama 35203
(205) 776-8975

Summary

Seven years as accounting supervisor and accountant with increasing responsibility and proven performance in a sophisticated computer-based accounting environment. Advanced training and successful experience in computerized accounting systems.

Experience and accomplishments

1988–present   Gulfstream Enterprises, Birmingham, Alabama

Staff accountant reporting to Controller of $20-million oil exploration company.

- Introduced, installed, and monitored new IBM ledger system. Trained accounting staff of 12 in its use.
- Identified significant error problem and instituted new system of financial reporting to correct it.
- My efforts resulted in a reduction in time and manpower for basic accounting functions and preparation of financial reports, and annual savings of $40,000.

1983–88   Davis Aerospace, Inc., Birmingham, Alabama

Accounting Supervisor in audit department of $50-million aerospace contractor. Received increasing responsibility with exceptional results while studying evenings for degree.

- Mastered full-charge and general ledger bookkeeping duties leading to supervision of six bookkeepers within one year.
- Instituted time- and cost-saving acccounting procedures.
- Reported directly to Auditor as company's chief computer systems troubleshooter.

Education: B.S., Accounting, University of Alabama, *magna cum laude*

Special Skills: Cobol I and II programming and systems analysis

References: Provided upon request, once mutual interest has been established.

ADVERTISING MANAGER

Regrettable

Margaret Fuller
543 Eagle's Nest Drive
White Plains, NY 10602
(914) 987-6432

Objective : To provide a large manufacturing,
•wholesaling, or retailing corporation with creative,
imaginative, sales-building advertising programs. **1**

Advertising and Promotion Experience

Advertising Manager; Contact Optical Centers,
Greenwich, CT, 1987-present. This $25 million company
has 29 outlets in Connecticut, New Jersey, and New
York providing eye examinations, eyeglasses, and
contact lenses at low cost. It has recently engaged
upon an aggressive expansion into three mid-Atlantic
states with 15 new mall locations. My duties consist
of: **2**

* Planning all advertising and promotion campaigns in
consultation with president and sales manager.

* Conducting all newspaper, billboard, and direct-
mail advertising on a budget of $1.25 million.

* Managing a staff of ten graphic designers,
copywriters, and assistants.

* Guiding the expansion program, including designing
special promotions.

* Utilizing Macintosh Desktop Publishing for graphics
in a variety of artwork genres.   **3**

Since joining this company in 1987, sales have
increased 200 percent. Tests show that my promotions
draw sales of 5 to 8 percent. Desire change because I
am ready for wider, higher echelon responsibility. **4**

Advertising Manager; Bronners Department Stores,
Columbus, Ohio, 1984-1987. This midwestern family
department store chain grosses $140 million a year.
As advertising manager, I made daily, Sunday,
holiday, and special event layouts for newspaper ads
and supervised preparation of copy and production; I
supervised the production of radio and TV
announcements. I prepared all stuffers for continuous
campaign mailings to charge customers. **5** Left to
gain higher responsibility at Contact Optical
Centers. **6**

Copywriter; Advance Advertising, Battle Creek,
Michigan, 1982-84. This agency had billings of over
$10 million, including the point-of-purchase contract
for Famous Breakfast Foods, the company's largest
account. I wrote all copy for the Famous displays.
Left for position of greater managerial
responsibility at Bronners.

Professional Training in Advertising and Sales   **8**

Certificate in Direct Mail Advertising. Academy of
Direct Mail Advertising, Advertising League of Ohio,
1985. While working for Bronners Department Stores, I
took an eight-week course and seminar in direct-mail
advertising. My model letters won first prize and
earned me a $500 award.

Certificate in Sales Promotion, School of Continuing
Education, University of Bridgeport, Bridgeport,
Connecticut, 1988. While working for Contact Optical,
I completed three continuing education courses in
sales, sales promotion, and advertising which led to

a special certificate. These courses were conducted
by leading authorities in all three fields.

<u>Bachelor of Science, Marketing</u>, Eastern Michigan
University, Ypsilanti, Michigan, 1982. Trained in all
phases of marketing with heavy emphasis on
advertising and promotion.

<u>Personal Data</u>   **9**

Parents owned small neighborhood department store in
Saline, Michigan, where I worked part-time and
summers during high school and college.

<u>References</u>   **10**

Mr. Robert Yotta, President; Contact Optical Centers,
1200 Corporate Towers, Greenwich, Connecticut 06830
(203) 866-0111

Ms. Angela Bronner, Vice-President; Bronners
Department Stores, 2400 Bronner Building, Columbus,
Ohio 43216

Mr. Frederick Neuman, Managing Partner; Advance
Advertising, 250 Otsego Way, Battle Creek, Michigan
(616) 663-3636

Comments

Margarget Fuller is on the right track—she's just riding in the wrong train. This resume is not the vehicle to get her a better position.

Although she emphasizes accomplishments in places, in general the resume is too long, too wordy, and contains unnecessary information. Its blocks of copy make it uninviting to read. Dates are buried within paragraphs, making it difficult to tell at a glance where she worked at a certain time.

Margaret is presenting herself as a creative communicator, capable of successfully promoting her employer's products. But her resume fails to prove it. It's not creative or concisely written. It doesn't represent her in a way that will get her hired.

Among the resume regrets here are:

1. **Tip 34, "Don't state an objective."**

   Margaret's objective is vague and nonspecific. The resume is not targeted to a specific position. This selling space is better used for a summary of qualifications.

2. **Tip 19, "Emphasize results, not responsibilities."**

   "My duties consist of" does not reveal how well she performed her duties nor what results were realized. She could have easily inherited an efficient department and a competent staff that knew what they were doing. Although she uses action verbs, such as "planning," "conducting," "managing," "guiding," and "designing," she doesn't emphasize her own effectiveness.

3. **Tip 39, "Don't overuse buzzwords."**

Though advertising insiders understand what Macintosh Desktop Publishing is, those who recognize good writing won't recognize it here. "Utilizing" is a poor verb. Just because you can utilize something doesn't mean you've mastered it, or even *use* it well.

"A variety of artwork genres" is abstract art on a portrait canvas. A better approach would be to list, in a section entitled "Special Skills and Knowledge," what desktop publishing software programs she has mastered.

4. **Tip 51, "Emphasize individual accomplishments."**

Resume readers will ask, "How did *she* help sales increase 200 percent?" When (if) they read on to learn that "Tests show that my promotions draw sales of 5 to 8 percent," they may well ask, "5 to 8 percent of what?" What is this an increase over?

The writer gives a reason for leaving, which is inappropriate. Further, she tells her reader *she* is ready for more responsibility, but she hasn't demonstrated how.

5. Once again, a list of duties without a shred of evidence that she contributed anything beyond mere effort. Efficiency and effectiveness can't be found, and a personneler won't look for them!

6. **Tip 35, "Don't give a reason for leaving previous jobs."**

7. **Tip 9, "Keep it short—no more than one page."**

As you'll see in the revised version, it is possible to edit close to a page of unnecessary verbiage and detail. The result is one concise page that *moves*.

8. This section on education breaks several important rules. It's far too long, "I's" the reader too much, and contains newsy, chatty data about some courses that mean little to most hirers.

9. Part-time work, even in a family business, belongs under a listing of experience and accomplishments.

10. **Tip 32, "Don't include names of references."**

    It's a waste of space, better used to market herself as a proven performer. "References are too precious to annoy, and you want to be able to contact them *first* and give them the scoop on the specific job and employer."

    Listing the current employer as a reference is suspicious. Hirers are accustomed to jobseekers requesting that their current employer *not* be contacted until an offer is accepted. Will this company be glad to be rid of this candidate?

    The revised resume that follows packages this promotional person into one powerful page that positions her properly.

Revised

Margaret Fuller
543 Eagle's Nest Drive
White Plains, New York 10602
(914) 987-6432

Summary

Advertising manager with eight years' in-house and agency experience with increased responsibility and scope. Idea person with proven ability to manage and lead a creative staff. Successful sales builder with media, direct-mail, point-of-purchase, and special promotions record.

Experience and Accomplishments

1987–present   Contact Optical Centers; Greenwich, Connecticut

Advertising manager with in-house staff of ten and annual budget of $1.25 million for 29-unit chain of optical centers grossing $25 million per year.

- Reduced media budget while significantly increasing exposure by instituting in-house agency.
- Negotiated, purchased, and installed five-station Macintosh Desktop Publishing network, which resulted in time and cost savings over traditional layout and typesetting while increasing in-house graphic and artistic capabilities.
- Created and controlled $.5 million promotional campaign to herald 15-unit expansion. As a result, first-quarter sales in new stores were 10 percent ahead of projections.

1984–87   Bronners Department Stores; Columbus, Ohio

Advertising manager for midwestern family department store chain grossing $140 million per year.

- Increased sales 8 percent in one year as a result of intensive direct-mail campaign to credit customers.

1982–84   Advance Advertising; Battle Creek, Michigan

Copywriter for Famous Breakfast Foods point-of-purchase promotions. Created nationwide "Tommy the Tiger" contest, which was credited with increasing market penetration by 5 percent.

Education: B.A., Marketing, Eastern Michigan University
Continuing education courses in direct mail and sales promotion

Special Skills & Knowledge: Aldus PageMaker®, MicrosoftWord®, MacDraw®, and MacWrite® programs. Skilled in operating and training others.

SYSTEMS ANALYST

Regrettable

<u>Daniel J. O'Keefe</u>

MIS professional with strong mainframe background

25 Sunnyside Lane
Walnut Creek, California 94596   (415)-965-5418

Objective: To serve as senior systems analyst
in computer center of a large
corporation, where my knowledge of
sophisticated systems, procedures, and
data base administration can be applied
to challenging problems.

EXPERIENCE   Five years' of high-level **1**   systems
design experience with THE BERKELEY
GROUP, Oakland, California, a large **1**
management consulting firm, as Manager,
Systems Design, 1985-present.

* Consulted with clients, reviewed problems and
developed proposals, specifying adaptive uses of
present hardware or new hardware to meet systems
needs. Designed new systems, oversaw installation and
initial operation, including orientation and training
of client personnel.

* Developed and implemented systems designs and
programs for client companies, which involved
close contact with senior management of client firms
to develop objectives, review constraints, and
recommend appropriate systems development. Built
mathematical models and programs.

REASON FOR LEAVING: To find a new position with a
larger corporation.

Five years of solid programming and systems design experience with ELECTRONIC SOLUTIONS CORP., Irvine, California, a small but important 1 software manufacturer, 1980-85.

* Led the team developing Write-Right™, a new word-processing program with grammar and spelling check features that has met with great market success.

* Redesigned ESC's order entry and shipping program, which resulted in 50% reduction in order-to-ship time.

EDUCATION   Master of Science (M.S.), Computer Sciences, University of California at Irvine, 1981. Thesis: "Computer Programming: A Systems Approach" published by University Press. Bachelor of Science, Electrical Engineering, California Polytechnic Institute, 1979. Full training in electrical engineering with heavy minor in mathematics. Learned mathematical model building in a trailblazing program that anticipated total systems approach to computer design.

Graduated summa cum laude, Member Phi Beta Kappa

AFFILIATIONS Member of three national professional societies:

National Society for Systems Analysts (NSSA)

American Association of Electric Engineers (AAEE)

American Association of Computer Scientists (AACS)

INTERESTS	Electronic Music, Programming Computer Games, Mountain Climbing, Philosophy, especially Epistemology
PERSONAL	Born in Alameda, California; attended California public schools, except for one year in Spain as an exchange student; speak and write fluent Spanish; single; no children, two dogs and a cat.
REFERENCES	Too numerous to list. A list of professional and academic references will be provided upon request.

Comments

This jobseeker has impressive credentials, but they're buried under an avalanche of too many words and too much unnecessary, inappropriate information. As with the first two resume writers, Daniel highlights "experience" and fails to shine the light on accomplishments that make him stand out.

1. **Tip 38, "Don't editorialize."**

   Our candidate violates this rule by referring to his "strong" background, "high-level" experience, and the "large" size of previous employers. None of these adjectives paints a clear picture of what he means. He should use his mathematical ability to quantify his achievements and make the reader understand his performance level.

   Daniel has given reasons for desiring a change from his present position, as well as information about his early childhood. Both are extraneous and take up valuable space.

   A crowded page layout where key dates and information don't jump out at the reader also works against him.

   His "personal interests" don't contribute much to understanding his professional competence. They're not unusual for a California computer scientist, but listing them could prompt a structured staff screener to label him a "kook." His resume will then be labeled "no interest."

   The candidate's qualifications are strong. They provide enough material for a powerful resume. The revision grabs the reader's attention with a strong career summary. Then it focuses on significant professional and academic achievements. It's short and specific—sure to make the phone ring with interview requests.

Revised

Daniel J. O'Keefe
25 Sunnyside Lane
Walnut Creek, California 94596
(415) 965-5418

Summary: Management Systems Analyst with 10-year successful track record in systems analysis, design, and programming for Fortune 500 client companies. Skillful problem solver with a strong foundation in computer sciences, electrical engineering, and mathematics.

Experience and Accomplishments

1985–present   *Manager, Systems Design*
                   The Berkeley Group, Oakland, California

Managed team of 20 programmers, systems designers, and computer engineers for management consulting firm with revenue of more than $10 million per year.

- Designed new systems, supervised installation and initial operation, including orientation and training of client personnel.
- Served as liaison with senior management of client firms to develop objectives, review constraints, and recommend appropriate systems design.

1980–85   *Systems Analyst*
                   Electronic Solutions Corporation, Irvine, California

Top programmer and systems design expert with this innovative software development company.

- Led the team developing Write-Right™, a new word-processing program with grammar and spelling check features that has met with great market success.
- Redesigned ESC's order entry and shipping program, which resulted in 50% reduction in order-to-ship time.

Education: M.S., Computer Sciences, University of California at Irvine
                      B.S.E.E., California Polytechnic Institute, minor in
                      mathematics

Honors: Graduated *summa cum laude*, Member *Phi Beta Kappa*

Publications: Master's Thesis: "Computer Programming for IBM
                      Mainframes: A Systems Approach" published by University
                      Press

Special Skills   IDMS/IDD
and Knowledge: MVS INTERNALS
                      VM PERFORMANCE TUNING
                      Fluent in Spanish

References: Provided on request, once mutual interest has been
                      established.

ATTORNEY

Regrettable

Bridget K. Lyons
BANK ATTORNEY

227 Upper Avenue, Des Moines, Iowa 50309 (515-865-9158)

Objective: To serve in the legal department, personal trust
department, or corporate trust department of a large
commercial bank.

Education: J.D., Drake University School of Law (evenings) 1989
Member of Bar, State of Iowa, 1990

B.S., Economics, Iowa State University, 1985 (earned
tuition and maintenance as night-shift typist for
legal department of First National Bank of Iowa)

Experience: Trust Officer, City Bank, Des Moines, 1989 to
present.

Main duties: Interview persons requesting personal
trust information; design personal trusts,
administer trusts, and speak to community groups

Manager, First National Bank, Des Moines, Iowa,
1985-89

Main duties: Hired as economic analyst, 1985;
promoted to assistant manager, Corporate Trust
Department, 1987, then to contract review manager,
legal department, 1988.

Left for more responsible position in larger bank

Clerk Typist, Legal Department, First National Bank,
1981-1985

Reason for Leaving: graduated from college, took
full-time position

References: Furnished upon request

Comments

Lawyer Lyons stuck to the one-page rule, but she won't budge a judge. She failed to elaborate on her achievements in five years of banking. The sketchy information she provides doesn't give any idea as to her leadership skill, managerial ability, or even professional credentials. This attorney needs help making her case before a job judge.

Bridget breaks the rules of content and style, as well. She fails to highlight dates and job titles to make it easy to follow her career. She gives an objective, reasons for leaving, and lists education first (rather than last).

As a lawyer, she should know better. The illogical format and ambiguities are, therefore, more devastating than those on previous resumes.

Revised

Bridget K. Lyons
227 Upper Avenue
Des Moines, Iowa 50309
(515) 865-9158

Career Summary: Attorney with economics background (including analysis), corporate trust management, and personal trust management achievement in major banks.

Professional Achievements

1989–present   *Trust Officer, City Bank, Des Moines, Iowa*

Manager of personal trust staff of 15, monitoring investments of $700 million. Established department policies, developed marketing and customer service programs, instituted community relations program, administered trusts, and controlled income to the bank in excess of $50 million. My policies and efforts resulted in increased visibility for new department and new revenue to the bank of $20 million in the first year of the department's operation.

1985–89   *First National Bank, Des Moines, Iowa*
Economic Analyst, 1985-1987

- Identified economic trends and environmental conditions affecting the bank and prevented losses from overemphasis in agricultural loans. My proposals and recommendations resulted in the diversification of the bank portfolio and overall strengthening of its financial picture. As a result of my success, promoted to

Assistant Manager, Corporate Trust Department, 1987-88

- Revised policies and established a trust account review system that resulted in an average 2 percent per year increase in return to clients and 24 percent annual increase in department revenue. Upon graduation from law school, promoted to

Contract Review Manager, Legal Department, 1988

- Created new, more effective policies for contract review, rewrote policy manual for contract preparation, and hired members of new department of contract writers.

Education: J.D., Drake University School of Law (evenings)
Member of the State Bar of Iowa
B.S., Economics, Iowa State University

References: Furnished upon request.

ENERGY MANAGER

Regrettable

Richard M. Austin, Jr.
2441 Lakeshore Road
Lake Forest, IL 60045
(312) 244-9152

RESUME

Objective: Energy Manager **1**

Summary: Sixteen years in the energy industry, with
increasing responsibility, including six years in
power plant process and operations, and ten years in
utility program management and marketing. Strong
technical background plus in-depth, current marketing
experience.

Background and experience include five years of one-
on-one contact with residential, commercial, and
industrial utility customers, advising them on energy
conservation methods, electric service requirements,
and utility program application.

Proven ability to target a need and develop programs
to meet that need, control and manage all facets of
program implementation, promotion, and follow-up.
Highly organized, efficient, and fast-paced. Hands-on
management style with excellent supervisory/team
leadership skills.

Highly effective in communicating and maintaining
rapport with such diverse groups as media
representatives, corporate executives, public
officials, government agencies, and consumers.

Excellent presentation and writing skills. **2**

Selected Achievements: As Administrator of
conservation programs with **3** annual budget of $1.5

million plus, responsible for ongoing program development. Redesigned and supervised production of new brochures and media campaigns. Acquired and managed 65,000-name mailing list. Developed and implemented new incentive program for field personnel and trade allies. Supervised creation and production of all promotion pieces, developed and led introductory seminars statewide, coordinated training seminars for in-house personnel, supervised and controlled follow-up mailings, and directed ongoing communications. As a result, at 6-month point program was 100% ahead of previous year's 8-month total and on target for 12-month goals.

Established and fostered relationships with equipment manufacturers to maximize cost-effectiveness to consumer of energy-efficient equipment through utility/manufacturer cost sharing.

Conducted situation analysis as integral part of formulating first corporate marketing plan.

Presently member of corporate team evaluating options available to Consolidated Utilities for new business opportunities.

Session Chair and Speaker, "The Conservation Debate," January, 1987 Demand-Side Management Seminar in Chicago, Illinois.

Member, task force for "Energy Solutions" Conference, November 1987, New Orleans, Louisiana. Session Chair and Speaker. Responsible for developing and presenting pre-conference workshop.

Co-chair, Customer Behavior & Preference Study commissioned by the Energy Research Institute in which conservation programs I designed are part of a central case study.

**Awards &
Associations:**
Edison Electric Institute National Writing Awards Program:
<u>1st Place</u>/Commercial Category, 1984
<u>2nd Place</u>/Industrial Category, 1983
<u>Honorable Mention</u>/Commercial Category, 1982

Illinois Energy Conservation Awards, 1986 and 1987

Chairman, Board of Directors, Lake Forest, Illinois Chamber of Commerce, 1984-85

**Employment
History:**
Senior Marketing Analyst, Marketing Services Department, Consolidated Utilities, 1987 to present

Administrator, Conservation & Load Management, Consolidated Utilities, Chicago, IL, 1986 to 1987

Energy Consultant, Consolidated Utilities, Northeastern Region, Evanston, Illinois 1980 to 1986

Nuclear Reactor Operator, U.S. Navy, 1974 to 1980

Education:
University of Chicago, M.B.A. with concentration in strategic management, 1989

Northern Illinois University, B.S. in Business Administration, <u>magna cum laude</u>, 1985

U.S. Naval Electronics, Nuclear, and Nuclear Prototype Schools

Comments

Richard's resume has a few distinct weaknesses. First, it's three pages—two pages too long. Second, it's written in functional format. Because of that, the reader doesn't really know when he worked where until near the bottom of the second page. That's too late.

Another problem is not with the resume but with the candidate. That job history is with one employer. By emphasizing accomplishments in each position and showing a progressive rise through the ranks, he can overcome this drawback.

Some other specific rules broken:

1. **Tip 34, "Don't state your objective."**

   By indicating a specific position title, he forecloses all other options.

2. **Tip 69, "Begin with a 'power summary.'"**

   Unique to the functional resume format is a long summary, such as the one written here. The reader gets bogged down in the language of this summary before he or she gets a clear picture of the candidate and his work history.

   In the revision that follows, Richard has tightened up the summary, using only what is necessary to get attention, and discarding the rest.

3. **Tip 7, "Summarize your experience, with the most recent employer and position first."**

   One advantage of the functional format is that it emphasizes achievements, but it does so in a way that confuses the reader. By taking the action vocabulary used and rearranging it chronologically in bulleted lists, a sharp picture emerges.

This candidate didn't get a bite with the regrettable resume for several years. After it was revised, he had three interviews within one month and three job offers.

Revised

Richard M. Austin, Jr.
2441 Lakeshore Drive
Lake Forest, Illinois 60045
(312) 244-9152

Summary: Sixteen years of utility management with increasing responsibility, including six years in power plant process and operations, and ten years in conservation program management and marketing. Strong technical background with current record of marketing achievement.

Experience and Accomplishments

1987 to present   *Senior Marketing Analyst*
Consolidated Utilities, Chicago, Ilinois

Senior staff member in corporate marketing services department responsible for forming company's competitive response and marketing strategy.

- Conducted situation analysis for CU's first marketing plan.
- Evaluated various load management technologies (e.g., cool storage, radio control devices); implemented, managed, and controlled pilot programs based on results of study.
- Key member of corporate task forces reporting to CEO and developing new business opportunities, competitive strategies, and better utilization of resources.

1986–1987   *Program Administrator, Conservation & Load Management*
Consolidated Utilities, Chicago, Illinois

Developed, managed, and controlled nationally recognized energy conservation program resulting in 5 MW of peak reduction per year. Managed annual budget of $1.5 million.

- Created, managed, and promoted successful trade ally incentive program comprised of over 1,000 distributors and manufacturers. Managed all direct mail and media advertising.
- Negotiated with contractor to provide communications, training, and fulfillment services for trade ally program and supervised all contractor activities.

1980–1986   *Energy Consultant*
Consolidated Utilities Eastern Region, Evanston, Illinois

Account executive for large commercial/industrial customers in region.
Supervised all customer service, load management, and conservation activities.

- Developed and conducted numerous technical educational programs for customers (e.g., motor and motor controls, power quality, etc.)
- Won Edison Electric Institute National Writing Awards 1982, 1983, and 1984 (Honorable mention, 2nd place, 1st place) for articles I wrote describing conservation and load management programs I devised for customers.

Education: M.B.A., University of Chicago
B.S., Business Administration, Northern Illinois
University, *magna cum laude*

References: Provided upon request, once mutual interest has been established.

MANAGEMENT TRAINEE

In Chapter 3, entitled "Special Problems," I gave specific guidelines for overcoming the circular dilemma of getting experience without having it.

Following are two versions of the resume of a recent college graduate. This jobgetter worked her way through college. After graduation, she took graduate-level courses before beginning her professional job search.

Examine both resumes closely. The first one is weak. Judging by the limping listings of education and college activities, this candidate doesn't stand out. How can she expect a screener to give her more than a "no interest" letter?

The revised resume takes a promotional approach, highlighting accomplishments both in school and at part-time jobs. It conveys the message: "I'm a proven producer, plus possess potent potential." Study the differences. I think you'll agree this jobgetter will be job jumping soon.

Regrettable

Gail M. Kowalski
4525 Meridian Street, Apt. 2
Indianapolis, IN 46206
(307) 765-9876

Objective: To be hired as management trainee in a
large company and eventually rise through the ranks
into general management.

Education: Purdue University Extension,
               Indianapolis
               22 credits toward MBA. Attended full
               time. 1988-89. Now attending part-time.
               Scheduled completion: June 1992.

               University of Notre Dame
               B.S. Business Administration, Summa Cum
               Laude

Experience: Hoosier Hospital Products
               Plainfield, Indiana
               1989-present

Customer Service Manager responsible for customer
order department staff of 15. Duties include document
routing from mailroom through production to shipping.
Coordinate inventory needs with production and
materials management departments.

               Accounting Department
               Indiana Aluminum Corporation
               North Webster, IN 46555
               1984-88

Part-time job while in college. Began as part-time
accounts receivable clerk (1984); promoted to
Supervisor, Accounts Receivable, 1986-88. Supervised
night-shift staff of three clerks. Suggested
computerized accounts receivable reporting mechanism;
helped improve collection of delinquent accounts.

References: Furnished upon request.

Revised

Gail M. Kowalski
4525 Meridian Street
Indianapolis, Indiana 46206
(307) 765-9876

Summary: *Management Trainee* with B.S. in Business Administration (*summa cum laude*) and 22 graduate credits toward M.B.A. Six years of professional management with increasing responsibility in full-time, part-time, and summer positions while attending college.

Experience and Achievements

1989–present   *Customer Service Manager*
Hoosier Hospital Products
Plainfield, Indiana

Plan and direct the activities of Customer Order Department staff of 15. Manage document routing from mail room through production to shipping. Plan inventory needs with production and materials management departments.

* Initiated project with manufacturing and purchasing to create more accurate finished goods reporting, which resulted in savings of $25,000 annually and significantly reduced order fulfillment time.

1984–88   *Supervisor, Accounts Receivable*
Indiana Aluminum Corporation
North Webster, Indiana

Began as part-time accounts receivable clerk, 1984. Promoted 1986 to supervisor of accounts receivable (night shift) in this manufacturing company with customer orders of $22 million per year.

* Developed computerized accounts receivable reporting mechanism; devised a system that reduced average collection time from 65 days to 42 days. Received bonus and commendation from corporate office as a result.

Education: Purdue University Extension, Indianapolis
M.B.A. program, 1988-89 full time; 1989–present, part-time. Scheduled completion: June 1992.

University of Notre Dame
B.S., Business Administration (*summa cum laude*)
* Maintained 3.9 GPA all four years while working an average of 30 hours per week.

References: Furnished upon request.

CONSTRUCTION SUPERVISOR

The next jobgetter has more than ten years' experience as a supervisor in the building trades, with a track record of success. In an increasingly competitive environment, however, his resume must give him an edge.

The first version lists his experience in chronological order, but makes the mistake of saving his *accomplishments* until the back page—where they may never get read.

The revised version replaces the unnecessary "Objective" statement with a crucial "Summary" statement, and condenses the resume into one page that spotlights his achievements.

The revision also eliminates the office address and the reason for leaving. It's always best to discuss a new position from home rather than from the office. The reason for leaving is better left for discussion during an interview.

Regrettable

Jonathan P. Dean

Home Address
16698 Hilltop Avenue
Allentown, PA 18101
(215) 559-0090

Office Address
Keystone Contruction Corp.
Downtown Office Towers
Allentown, PA 18101
(215) 555-1212

OBJECTIVE: Supervisory position in residential or commercial construction

EXPERIENCE:

1989-present   Keystone Construction Corporation, Allentown, PA

Construction Supervisor for Penns Woods residential development of 150 new homes and condominium units. Hired and supervised crew of 22, interpreted and implemented architects' building and site plans.

1987-89   Lehigh Valley Development, Mount Bethel, PA

Master Carpenter and Crew Leader. Hired as journeyman carpenter, then promoted to master carpenter and crew leader on 500,000 square-foot retail/office center in Mount Bethel. Directed layout, exterior fabrication, and interior installation.

1985-87   Craft Building and Supply, Chester, PA

Journeyman carpenter assisting master carpenters on new construction and renovation to both commercial and residential structures. Also learned purchasing and estimating.

1981-85   Seargent, U.S. Army Corps. of Engineers

Specialized training in construction led to
equivalent of journeyman carpenter certification.
Crew leader for various construction projects on Army
bases throughout U.S.

EDUCATION: U.S. Army Engineering School, Maryland,
              Certificate in Carpentry

              Great Lakes Institute, Erie,
              Pennsylvania. Contruction Trades
              Certificate (one-year)

              Lehigh Valley Technical High School
              Four years of study in carpentry,
              drafting, and mechanical design

SKILLS: Fully qualified in all phases of general
carpentry. Thoroughly acquainted with lumber. Able to
estimate construction costs for developing tracts.
Adept in building layout and all surveying tools.
Knowledgeable about masonry, plumbing, electricity,
heating, air conditioning and landscaping.

Revised

Jonathan P. Dean
16698 Hilltop Avenue
Allentown, Pennsylvania 18101
(215) 559-0090

Summary: Construction Supervisor with 10 years of accomplishment in residential and commercial projects. Adept at estimating, purchasing, controlling materials, and executing building plans. Proven ability to select qualified workers and motivate them.

Experience and Achievements

1989–present *Construction Supervisor*
Keystone Construction Corporation, Allentown, Pennsylvania

For Penns Woods residential development of 150 homes and condominium units:
- Estimated costs, interpreted architects' plans, ordered materials, created construction schedules, hired and supervised crew of 22. Project to be completed ahead of schedule.
- Made successful presentation to lender for project refinancing, which resulted in savings of $50,000.

1987–89 *Master Carpenter and Crew Leader*
Lehigh Valley Development, Mount Bethel, Pennsylvania

For 500,000-square-foot retail/office center in Mount Bethel.
- Directed layout, exterior fabrication, and interior installation. Included heating, ventilation & air conditioning (HVAC), plumbing, electric, wall and floor coverings.

1985–87 *Journeyman Carpenter/Estimator*
Craft Building and Supply, Chester, Pennsylvania

Assisted master carpenters on construction or renovation of both commercial and residential structures. Learned and assumed responsibility for purchasing and estimating of jobs.

1981–85 *Sergeant, U.S. Army Corps of Engineers*
Crew leader for various construction projects on Army bases throughout U.S.

Education:	**U.S. Army Engineering School, Fort Belvedere, Maryland** Certificate in Carpentry (Journeyman Equivalent)
	Great Lakes Institute, Erie, Pennsylvania Contruction Trades Certificate (one-year)
	Lehigh Valley Technical High School, Mount Bethel, Pennsylvania Classes and practical experience in carpentry, drafting, and mechanical design
References:	Provided on request, once mutual interest has been established.

CHIEF HOSPITAL ADMINISTRATOR

Chapter 2 offered resume rules for the upper rungs. In the next two resumes, we see the same chief hospital administrator in two different ways.

The first resume demonstrates that this individual has excellent professional and academic credentials. But the second resume reveals more in less space.

The second resume also reflects a knowledge of the market and what the consumer will buy. Its presentation reflects an accurate perception of the search process.

The revision shows the writer knows that the hospital's board of directors is looking for an administrator who can do more than routine management tasks—a director who can motivate the hospital's professional and administrative staff to accomplish their goals.

Regrettable

5465 Sandia Way, Albuquerque, NM 87114
(505) 345-6723

HOSPITAL ADMINISTRATOR

Professional Objective

To serve as Chief Administrator of a large general
hospital.

Experience

SANDIA GENERAL HOSPITAL   ALBUQUERQUE, NM
Acting Chief Administrator, 1989 to present

Direct all activities of this 200-bed hospital,
reporting to the Board of Governors, in the absence
of permanent Chief Administrator, who will return to
hospital after two years' sabbatical in December.

Oversee hiring, training, and management of all
nonprofessional personnel. Directed hospital budget,
instituted cost-containment measures, expedited
collections and third-party reimbursement. Initiated
private capital campaign, which has resulted in $2
million increase in hospital endowment. Represent
hospital in all community affairs. Established new
community health projects.

ALBUQUERQUE VETERANS HOSPITAL   ALBUQUERQUE, NM
Assistant Hospital Administrator, 1985-89

Designed, implemented and administered new
computerized admissions system when hospital was
renovated in 1985. Put in charge of $20 million
three-year renovation project. Lobbied Congress and
the Veteran's Administration for funding, solicited
bids for project, negotiated contract, and worked

closely with contractors to bring renovation project
in at bid and on schedule. As hospital's training
officer, interpreted Veteran's Administration
training policies and developed professional and
nonprofessional improvement programs.

Education

UNIVERSITY OF TEXAS   AUSTIN, TX

Master of Hospital Administration, 1982-85

Three-year program, including one-year administrative
residence at M.D. Anderson Cancer Center, Houston,
TX. Graduated with honors. Academic program included
the following courses:

Hospital Management
Medical Care Administration
Computerized Hospital Accounting Systems
Case Studies in Hospital Design
Community Relations and Fund-Raising
Hospital Budgeting
Professional and Nonprofessional Personnel Management

UNIVERSITY OF NEW MEXICO   ALBUQUERQUE, NM

Bachelor of Science, (Biology Major)   1978-82

Dean's List every semester. Graduated cum laude with
3.5 average. Attended on National Merit full-tuition
scholarship. Worked at Community Hospital as
admissions clerk part-time to pay living expenses, as
a result of which work I decided on graduate training
and a professional career in hospital administration.

SPECIAL SKILLS   Speak and read fluent Spanish &
& KNOWLEDGE: English
                 Persuasive public speaker and
                 presenter

Revised

Consuelo V. Alvarez
5465 Sandia Way
Albuquerque, New Mexico 87114
(505) 345-6723

Summary: Graduate degree and five years' experience in hospital administration, including acting chief admininstrator. Effective manager with unique ability to train, motivate, and direct people. Successful record in capital improvement, management of renovation projects, installation of computerized management systems, and development of training programs. Problem solver with human relations skills.

Accomplishments

1989–present   *Acting Chief Administrator*
Sandia General Hospital, Albuquerque
Directed all activities of this 200-bed hospital, reporting to the Board of Governors in the absence of permanent Chief Administrator during his two-year sabbatical.
- Managed all nonprofessional personnel. Developed and administered hospital budget, instituted cost-containment measures, expedited collections and third-party reimbursement. Initiated private capital campaign, which has resulted in $2 million increase in hospital endowment. Represented hospital in all community affairs. Established three new community health projects, which significantly enhanced hospital's presence in community.

1985–89   *Assistant Hospital Administrator*
Albuquerque Veterans Hospital
- Designed, implemented, and administered computerized admissions system.
- Directed $20-million three-year renovation project. Lobbied Congress and the Veteran's Administration for funding, solicited bids for project, negotiated contract, and worked closely with contractors to complete renovation project at bid, on schedule.
- As hospital's training officer, interpreted Veteran's Administration training policies. Developed effective professional and nonprofessional improvement programs.

Education: *Master of Hospital Administration,* University of Texas
(Degree of Distinction)
Bachelor of Science, University of New Mexico, Biology
Major, graduated *cum laude*

Special Skills   Speak and read fluent Spanish and English
and Knowledge: Persuasive public speaker and presenter

OFFICE MANAGER

The final resume presented, critiqued, and revised is for someone who bills herself as a "Person Friday." Her resume is neat, attractive, and arranged chronologically with all the important data readily available. She makes a few mistakes, which, while not crucial, could have her spending many Fridays waiting for the weekend want ads. Can you tell what they are?

Regrettable

MONICA L. SHORT   General Office
2905 Jefferson Way   Typing, Word-Processing
Columbia, Maryland 21043   Bookkeeping, Telephone
(301) 239-6271

EFFICIENT, EXPERIENCED PERSON FRIDAY ready to take
full responsibility for operating general office of
small manufacturing, retail, or service firm.
Cheerful, attractive, and accustomed to one-person
office operations. Available because of present
employer's relocation to another state.

Experience

Chesapeake Shipping Company   Baltimore, MD

Office manager and supervisor, staff of three clerks.
Wrote shipping schedule and scheduled work of 45
warehouse and dock employees. Helped plan shipping
routes. Prepared payroll. Supervised bookkeeping,
typing, telephone, and office reception.

1987-present

Mid-States Stamping Plant   Baltimore, MD

One-person office force for this small manufacturer
of auto engine parts. Administered payroll, benefits,
and recordkeeping for 50 employees. Billed customers,
made bank deposits, ordered office supplies, typed
all correspondence, received callers, answered
telephone, filed, and kept records for tax returns.

1982-1987

Kramer's Furs   Washington, D.C.

Part-time office assistant for this 10-employee
exclusive fur retailer. Typed, filed, checked in new
merchandise, kept inventory records, assisted on
selling floor when needed.

1976-1982

EDUCATION: Katharine Gibbs Executive Secretarial
Course

What's wrong with this resume?

Let's review the rules that are broken:

Tip 35, "Don't give a reason for leaving previous jobs."

I've gone over this "don't" before. Anything you say talks you out of an interview.

Tip 40, "Don't give any clues to age."

Calling herself a "Person Friday" dates Monica. She appears to be a well-intentioned amateur. It's a carryover from the sexist "Girl Friday" title. "Office manager" is a much more professional, contemporary job title.

Referring to herself as "cheerful and attractive" in her summary may hurt Monica, too. Employers are barred from judging applicants on their looks, but they do it all the time. An enlightened human resourcer knows better, though. He or she just won't pass it along.

Aside from these mistakes, the resume is concise, clear, and compelling. It needs just a bit of rearranging of information to make it a *super* resume.

Revised

Monica L. Short
2905 Jefferson Way
Columbia, Maryland 21043
(301) 239-6271

Efficient Office Manager with 15 years' experience. Proven ability to supervise office of small manufacturing, retail, or service firm. Personable, well groomed, and accomplished as a one-person office force or directing a clerical staff.

Experience and Accomplishments

1987–present *Clerical Supervisor*
Chesapeake Shipping Company, Baltimore, Maryland

Office manager of staff with three clerks. Scheduled work of 45 warehouse and dock employees. Helped plan shipping routes. Prepared payroll. Supervised bookkeeping, typing, and office reception. Evaluated and purchased word-processing software for office computers. Trained employees to use it.

1982–1987 *Office Manager*
Mid-States Stamping Plant, Baltimore, Maryland

One-person office force for this small manufacturer of auto engine parts. Administered payroll, benefits, and recordkeeping for 50 employees. Billed customers, made bank deposits, ordered office supplies, typed all correspondence, received callers, answered telephone, filed, and maintained records for tax purposes.

1976–1982 *Part-Time Office Assistant*
Kramer's Furs, Washington, D.C.

Typed, filed, checked in new merchandise, kept inventory records, and assisted on selling floor when needed at this exclusive fur retail establishment.

Education: Katharine Gibbs Executive Secretarial Course

Special Skills and Knowledge: Full-charge bookkeeping, word-processing (MultiMate® & WordPerfect®), typing 100 wpm.

References: Furnished upon request.

132

Conclusion

There you have it. *Jeff Allen's Best: The Resume.* All 100 techniques presented in this book were incorporated into the revised resumes of the nine candidates presented in this section. The result: interviews!

Did their qualifications change? Of course not. We just recognized that a resume is nothing more than a direct-mail marketing device—the "facts" are far less important than the *presentation.*

When you consider that even the nine "regrettable" samples were better than the average resume, you can see how revising them gets results. All you need is to get your foot in the interviewer's door.

In *Jeff Allen's Best: Get the Interview* and *Jeff Allen's Best: Win the Job,* we'll get the rest of your body in there—and *out* with the "best" *offer!*

Endnotes

1. Jackson, Tom, *The Perfect Resume*. New York: Doubleday, 1981, page 73.

2. Allen, Jeffrey G., J.D., C.P.C., *The Perfect Job Reference*. New York: John Wiley & Sons, 1990.

3. Allen, Jeffrey G., J.D., C.P.C., *Jeff Allen's Best: Get the Interview*. New York: John Wiley & Sons, 1990.

4. Foxman, Loretta D., *The Executive Resume Book*. New York: John Wiley & Sons, 1989, page 8.

5. *Ibid.*, pages 41–42.

6. *Ibid.*, page 46.

7. Allen, Jeffrey G., J.D., C.P.C., *Surviving Corporate Downsizing*. New York: John Wiley & Sons, 1988.

8. Allen, Jeffrey G., J.D., C.P.C., *The Perfect Job Reference*. New York: John Wiley & Sons, 1990.

9. Allen, Jeffrey G., J.D., C.P.C., and Jess Gorkin, *Finding the Right Job at Midlife*. New York: Simon & Schuster, 1985, page 9.

10. *Ibid.*, page 64.

11. *Ibid.*, page 13.

12. *Ibid.*, pages 13–14.

13. Foxman, pages 64–65.

14. Foxman, Pages 66–67.

Bibliography

Allen, Jeffrey G. J.D., C.P.C., and Jess Gorkin, *Finding the Right Job at Midlife*. New York: Simon & Schuster, 1985.

Allen, Jeffrey G., J.D., C.P.C., *Jeff Allen's Best: Get the Interview*. New York: John Wiley & Sons, 1990.

Allen, Jeffrey G., J.D., C.P.C., *Jeff Allen's Best: Win the Job*. New York: John Wiley & Sons, 1990.

Allen, Jeffrey G., J.D., C.P.C., *The Perfect Job Reference*. New York: John Wiley & Sons, 1990.

Allen, Jeffrey G., J.D., C.P.C., *Surviving Corporate Downsizing*. New York: John Wiley & Sons, 1988.

Foxman, Loretta D., *The Executive Resume Book*. New York: John Wiley & Sons, 1989.

Jackson, Tom, *The Perfect Resume*. New York: Doubleday, 1981.

Lewis, Adele, *The Best Resumes for Scientists and Engineers*. New York: John Wiley & Sons, 1988.

Tepper, Ron, *Power Resumes*. New York: John Wiley & Sons, 1989.

Index